Best Wishes Jasmin -

Joan McWilliams

People Are Talking About
Joan McWilliams' Books ...

Creating Parenting Plans That Work

The Creating Parenting Plans That Work booklet is
terrific—what a treasure of information about the needs
of children and the damage of high conflict.

> Carla Garrity, PhD.
> The Neuro-Developmental Center and
> Co-author of *Children of Divorce*

If you need a Parenting Plan, Joan McWilliams' book is
a must. Easy to use and read, full of useful tips and
advice. Highly recommended

> Isolina Ricci, PhD.,
> Author of *Mom's House, Dad's House*

D0168385

I give a copy of *Creating Parenting Plans That Work* to all my clients when they first come in the office. I tell them that the book was written by a lawyer who not only knows what she's talking about, she also helped draft the Parental Responsibilities Act! The book puts all the important information in one easy-to-handle spot. When I meet with the client the next time they come in, they understand Parenting Plans, and, quite often, have started to draft their own! *Creating Parenting Plans That Work* is a tremendous help—saves time and money!

Mark Leonard, Esq.
Brownstein Hyatt Farber Schreck LLP

The Peace Finder:
Riley McFee's Quest for World Peace

The PeaceFinder shows you how to become the peace that you wish to see in the world.

Arun Gandhi
President, M.K. Gandhi Institute for
Nonviolence

A delightful poem with a message our world has never needed more. For every person who has thrown up his hands and asked "But what can I do?" *The Peace Finder* offers a simple yet profound answer. Join Riley McFee on his quest and become part of the solution. It may just change your life.

> Stephanie Kane
> Author of *Blind Spot, Quiet Time* and *Seeds of Doubt: A Crime Novel*

Author Joan McWilliams has given us a grand idea in this charming, enlightening, and important book. Peace—enduring world peace—is within the reach of all of us; but, she says, we need to embrace that concept more than we entertain the rush to war as our default problem solving. Her straight-forward idea is told in a poem about a gifted young child (purity and innocence) finding his way through skeptics and nay-sayers to the mindful and conscious attainment of peace.

The world can no longer afford the catastrophic economic and psychological consequences of war and violence. McWilliams points out that finding peace is imperative to our survival and shows a positive way to contribute our energy to the solution. A life without violence? *The Peacefinder* shows us it is possible.

> Mary Beth Starzel
> Writer/Editor

Parenting Plans
For Families
After Divorce

Including A Special Section on
Child-Inclusive Parenting Plans

Also by Joan McWilliams

The PeaceFinder: Riley McFee's Quest for World Peace
Creating Parenting Plans That Work

Parenting Plans For Families After Divorce

Joan H. McWilliams, Esq.

McWilliams Mediation Group LTD
PO Box 6216
Denver, CO 80206

Books may be purchased in quantity and/or for special sales by contacting the publisher or author through the website:
www.McWilliamsMediation.com
email address: *Joan@McWilliamsMediation.com*
address: McWilliams Mediation Group LTD
PO Box 6216, Denver, CO 80206
Or, by contacting your local bookstore.

Cover Design: NZ Graphics, Nick Zelinger
Layout Design: WESType Publishing Services, Inc., Ronnie Moore
Editing: The Book Shepherd, Judith Briles, and Editing By John, John Maling
Cover Photo: Stephanie Secrest
Publisher: McWilliams Mediation Group LTD

Joan H. McWilliams, Esq.
Parenting Plans For Families After Divorce

Library of Congress Control Number: 2011902640

ISBN: 978-0-9768663-0-5
10 9 8 7 6 5 4 3 2 1

1. Divorce   2. Parenting   3. Family

Printed in Canada

This book is dedicated to
the parents and children of divorce
who recognize the importance
of maintaining a peaceful and
vibrant *Post-Divorce Family*.

Contents

Contents

Contents

PART THREE:
Making Your
Parenting Plan Work   117

A Letter to Parents

Thank you for giving me the opportunity to share the *Post-Divorce Family Model*™ with you. As part of The *New* American Way of Divorce, the *Post-Divorce Family Model* seeks to replace the traditional approach to divorce that does not support you, your children or your family. It relies on new ideas and processes by which you can preserve your family (even after your divorce) rather than damage or destroy it. I use the word d*ivorce* throughout the book to include the dissolution of any relationship, including those of unmarried couples.

You won't find the term, *Post-Divorce Family*, in any law book, and you won't hear most judges discuss it. When people divorce, they make provisions for their children, but they lose sight of the big picture. The truth is that even though you and the other parent will live in separate houses and lead separate lives, both of you will continue to be part of your original family, and that family unit needs to be consciously restructured, loved and nurtured.

Relying on this philosophy, the new *Post-Divorce Family Model*:

- Starts very early in the divorce process— before love turns to acrimony.

- Acknowledges that, while your family will take on a different form after your divorce, it will still exist and needs to be nourished.

- Discards the "one size fits all" approach to divorce.

- Recognizes that each family has different attributes and challenges.

- Provides creative processes and solutions that strive to meet the needs of each family member.

- Shows you how to design your own *Post-Divorce Family*—you and the other parent make the decisions—not the judge. This saves time, money and reduces stress.

- Suggests that you follow the five "Cs":

  1. **Commit** *to your children*—they must *always* come first.

  2. **Compartmentalize** *your anger*—take it away from the children.

  3. **Communicate** *with the other parent*— you still have to talk about the kids.

  4. **Consider** *the ideas of your children*— they will talk—are you listening?

  5. **Change** *your approach to conflict*—learn to peacefully resolve old problems.

In addition, the *Post-Divorce Family Model* reminds you to calm yourself and laugh a lot, give yourself regular hugs, and comfort all members of your family—they will each grieve and need your love and attention.

Keep the Celtic tree in mind. I have placed it on the cover and throughout *Parenting Plans For Families After Divorce*. It is a symbol of strength, love, connection and renewal. I hope it will provide support for you in your divorce.

Most importantly, contemplate peace in your *Post-Divorce Family*. Visualize it. Act on it. Make it a reality.

Best wishes for a successful journey. It will be worth all the effort.

Joan McWilliams, Esq.

Introduction

What Is This Book About?

This book is about designing a plan for your family after divorce that will enable you to help your children live in the two worlds that you are about to create. It will help you find answers to the questions you have about co-parenting with the other parent. It will show you how to create a *Parenting Plan* that will benefit you, your children, and your *Post-Divorce Family*.

When you're in the middle of a divorce, it's hard to think about anything but survival. You may find yourself in psychological, emotional, spiritual and financial places that you never before imagined. But, there are solutions to every problem, and this book will help you find many of those solutions.

How Can We Avoid Hurting Our Children?

You can begin by understanding that divorce does not have to be angry and expensive. Believe it or not, you can turn it into a positive experience. But— you have to work at it. If you succeed, you, your children, and your *Post-Divorce Family* will reap enormous benefits. It is perhaps the greatest gift you can give.

If you are going through a divorce, it is likely that you will experience pain—perhaps more pain that you have ever endured. But, if you allow it, you will learn from your pain. You will be angry. It's part of the grieving process. What's critical is that you take your anger away from your children and away from your co-parenting efforts. Smart couples control their emotional and financial divorce expenditures. Here are a variety of comments from some of my *smart* clients:

> *Once we were able to set aside our anger and focus on the children, my former husband and I both appreciated that we were on a good path for the kids. Working out our differences saved us a bundle of money. We didn't have to go to court, and we taught ourselves to work with the children even though we live in separate homes and don't like each other very much.*

I can't forget that my wife betrayed me. I was furious, and I was devastated. But, I have to admit that she's a good mother. I have worked hard to put my pain in a place away from the children and away from my parenting relationship with my ex-wife. We both really try hard to work together so the kids can have a normal life.

My former partner and I try to communicate directly with each other. It makes me crazy. But, we have learned that sending messages through the children puts too much responsibility on their shoulders, and they often mess up the message so the other parent gets the wrong information. Even though it's really irritating to talk to her, I know that it's less expensive than always going to court or mediation, and it's better for the kids.

My wife and I put a divorce team together. We chose attorneys who respected each other and chose a mediator who was knowledgeable and could work well with all of us. We used one joint expert who valued my business. We stayed in control of the process and reached an agreement that worked for us and for our three children. Years later, even though we have both remarried, my former wife and I celebrate holidays together with the children and remain good friends.

We have had to learn how to do everything differently. It's been hard. I thought I would be rid of my wife when I divorced her. Now I find that we have to constantly talk about the children. But, it's worth it. The kids are doing great.

If I had it to do all over again, I would insist that we approach the process of divorce differently. We did it the old fashioned way—adversarial lawyers, child family investigators, psychologists, several financial experts. We were angry when we started the divorce, but we were angrier when we finished. We could have saved so much time, stress and money if we had only cooperated with each other. We still would have used the experts, but we could have toned it down a lot. It would have been better for the children too.

I now realize that the only thing I can control is my attitude. I can't control my former husband, but I can maintain my composure and keep working towards a peaceful and positive post-divorce relationship with him regardless of how he reacts to me. I have vowed that I will not be deterred by his negative attitude. It gets hard sometimes, and I have to always focus. But, that's what it's about. Focus on the end result: raising healthy and productive children.

My husband and his former wife, Jane, were divorced ten years ago. They had two sons. We married eight years ago and have a five-year-old son. My husband stayed in the former marital house, and Jane bought a house just one block away. I think we are an example of an amazingly successful blended family, but it hasn't been easy. What we have found is this: if we always put the children first, the anger and fear dissipate. Our reward: the children are happy. This year, my husband even put Jane on his country club membership so she could go to the club with the boys. Pretty remarkable, think.

Our judge told us, "When you take a swing at the other parent, you'll hit your children." He was right.

Couples rarely experience a perfect divorce. But, when your children are involved, it's worth trying to work with the other parent to make the process as good as possible. You can leave the other parent but not your family.

Why Write This Book Now?
What's Changed?

I wrote *Creating Parenting Plans That Work* in 1998. I was inspired by the fact that the Colorado Legislature had just passed The Parental Responsibilities Act. I worked hard with other attorneys and mental health professionals to draft this Act and steer it through the Legislature. It literally changed the language of divorce in Colorado.

With this legislation, we struck the word, "custody" from the law. "Custody" was often used by parents to indicate that they were the "better parent" or that they had the ownership and control of their children. We replaced "custody" with the term, "parental responsibilities," which is an umbrella term that includes *Parenting Time* (formerly "visitation") and major *Decision Making*. *Parenting Plans* were required to be submitted to the Court. The Act reflected an enormous change in the law and a new and more positive approach to divorce. As a result, I felt compelled to share some of the successful ideas and techniques that I had developed in my mediation practice.

Now, it's time to rewrite the 1998 version of *Creating Parenting Plans That Work* because, once again, there have been significant changes in our ideas about divorce and the needs of the children.

These are important concepts that should be made available to divorcing parents. Let me explain.

- First, in the last thirteen years, there has been a positive shift in people's approach to divorce. Why? I believe that it's because (1) parents are more knowledgeable (or are willing to learn new facts and ideas) about how to avoid harming their children; (2) they recognize that they can divorce the other parent but not their family; and (3) they are more cautious with their money.

  In my experience, people are now actively seeking to understand their role as divorced parents and to find new ways to create healthy co-parenting relationships. They recognize that there are physical, emotional and financial benefits to becoming co-parenting partners in the business of raising healthy and productive children. They accept the idea that they have a *Post-Divorce Family* that will continue to function long after their decree is entered by the court. And, most parents now understand that violence, conflict, alienation and

abandonment indelibly scar their
children, and they will no longer tolerate
that behavior. *Parenting Plans For Families
After Divorce* acknowledges these shifts
and provides fresh ideas for navigating
your way through the process.

- Second, we now appreciate the
importance of finding safe and
appropriate ways to include children's
ideas in *Parenting Plans*. We know from
interviews with adult children of divorce
that their exclusion from the family
divorce crisis caused them pain when
they were younger and continues to
cause them pain in their adulthood.

    Children are stakeholders in the
family, and parents are finding ways to
give them a voice in the process. Are
there limits to the ways in which you
include your children? Yes—there must
be limits. Chapter 11 will show you how
to create a *Child-Inclusive Parenting Plan*
that will be safe and age-appropriate for
YOUR children.

- Third, there is a greater awareness of
nontraditional families including never

married parents, gay/lesbian/
transgender/bisexual parents,
multicultural/ multiracial parents, and
non-parents as parents. We are learning
to recognize the challenges that parents
of special needs children face. We
are seeing nontraditional living
arrangements in which parents are
choosing to live together after the divorce
because they can't afford to live
separately. Additionally, we find that
some parents are living as though they
are divorced but do not get a formal
Decree of Dissolution, which allows a
non-working or uninsurable parent to
remain on the other's health insurance.
Each of these situations must be
accommodated in the *Parenting Plan*.
They are discussed in Chapter 7.

• And fourth, don't forget technology.
Since 1998, there has been an explosion
in our ability to access people and
information. We now have cell phones,
texting, the Internet, Skype, Twitter,
Facebook, blogs, and a myriad of other
new developments. These advances
make communicating with children so

much easier than it used to be. But, there are also dangers, and parents must cooperate with each other to make sure that their children are not placed at risk through the use of technology. Special guidelines are included in Chapter 6.

> **These changes led me to conclude that the first edition of *Creating Parenting Plans That Work* needed a major facelift—new information, new ideas, and new approaches to parenting after divorce, i.e. The *New* American Way of Divorce. You will want to include some of these concepts in your *Parenting Plan*.**

Can Anyone Use This Book?

Yes! However, if your particular situation involves issues of domestic violence, mental instability, abuse or neglect, you must consider working with professionals in the legal, mental health or law enforcement communities. In all instances, you must protect yourself and your children.

PART ONE

Creating a *Parenting Plan* for Your Family

Chapter 1

Parenting Plan Q & A—

Simple Questions/Simple Answers

What Are the Basic Parts of a *Parenting Plan*?

A *Parenting Plan* is a design for the way you will raise your children after you are separated or divorced. In many ways, it is like a business plan. It will have a beginning, middle, and an end. Some parts of it will be included because they reflect your aspirations, and some parts will be included because they are required by law.

For the beginning, you might want to start by writing a *Family Mission Statement* that defines your family's vision and goals. What will your family look like after the divorce? You will find that a *Family Mission Statement* will help you maintain focus—even in the most difficult times of your divorce. Although a *Family Mission Statement* is not required by law to be in your *Parenting Plan* and is aspirational rather than mandatory, it has proven to be so helpful, you will want to consider taking the time to create one. *Family Mission Statements* are described in Chapter 2.

For the middle part of your *Parenting Plan*, you will want to include a section on the way you and the other parent will make major decisions for your children. Some states refer to this as *legal custody*. In this book, I call it *Decision-Making*. The major decisions that you will make for your children include health, education, and general welfare. There may be other areas such as religion, therapy, participation in high-risk activities and the choice of day-care providers that are important to you and that you will want to include in your *Plan*. *Decision-Making* is explained in Chapter 3.

You will also include a section on *Parenting Time*. This section will describe how the children will spend time with you and with the other parent. Some states call this *visitation*. You will want to consider monthly, holiday, and vacation *Parenting Time Schedules*, and identify a *Schedule* that best meets your child's developmental needs and is in your child's best interests. *Parenting Time Schedules* are discussed in Chapter 4.

The last part of your *Parenting Plan* will include the ways that you will resolve disagreements. In Chapter 10, you will learn about *Dispute Resolution* and the methods that you can use if you run into problems. You will want to choose a method that is most likely to help you and the other parent reach resolution of the particular issues with which you are working.

These are the basic parts of your *Parenting Plan*: A *Family Mission Statement*, guidelines for *Decision-Making*, a *Parenting Time Schedule*, and a method of *Dispute Resolution*. They are each important and will contribute greatly to the success of your *Post-Divorce Family*.

> In drafting your **Parenting Plan**, always consider the best interests of your children and give paramount consideration to their physical, developmental, mental, and emotional needs. Don't forget about your needs and the needs of the other parent—they must be considered too. And ... identify the needs of your **Post-Divorce Family**. Your children will always be part of their original family.

Can We Add Other Provisions to Our *Parenting Plan*?

Yes. You may want to include additional sections or provisions that apply to your particular situation. A

Parenting Plan can be very complex or very simple. You should design it specifically for your family's needs.

When you're working on your *Parenting Plan*, consider special things or activities that you want your children to have. Many of these are discussed in Chapters 3 and 4, but you can include any provision that is in the best interests of your children.

Be sure to discuss how you will communicate with the other parent (Chapter 5) and how you will jointly limit the children's use of cell phones, the Internet, TV, social networks and the like (Chapter 6). You will also want to consider whether or not you want to ask your children for their ideas (Chapter 11), and you will want to think about the financial needs of your kids and how you will pay for them (Chapter 8). The needs of nontraditional families are discussed in Chapter 7.

Creating a *Parenting Plan* might seem overwhelming at first. But, if you divide the task into manageable sections, you can build your *Plan* step-by-step. If possible, work with the other parent. If you and the other parent can't do it without help, hire a mediator or work with your lawyers or other professionals. The most effective *Parenting Plans* are the ones that are designed by both parents.

You are getting a divorce, but your children aren't. They need both parents. So, create a *Parenting Plan* that works for you and your *Post-Divorce Family*.

Do We Need to Write a *Parenting Plan*?

Many states have laws that require parents to draft a *Parenting Plan* when they get divorced or become legally separated. The most effective *Plans* are those written jointly by both parents because, if you mutually decide what is best for your children, you will each be more likely to adhere to the principles in your *Plan*. If you can't work directly with the other parent, hire a mediator to assist you or work with your lawyers, therapist, minister, doctor or other professionals that you trust. Each parent may submit a separate *Plan* to the court for its consideration or you can submit a joint *Plan*.

Be sure to review the law in your state. As a general rule, if a *Parenting Plan* is not submitted or if the court does not approve your *Plan*, the judge may be required to write one for you. Either way, the *Parenting Plan* will become an order of the court and will be enforceable by the court.

A **Parenting Plan** has enormous personal
and legal significance. It will affect your
life and the lives of your children.
If possible, use this legal requirement
as an opportunity to retain control and
define your parental responsibilities
after the divorce or separation. You
have only one chance to raise your
children. Don't waste it. Help your
children receive the best from both of
their parents.

When Should We Write a *Parenting Plan*?

You can write a *Parenting Plan* at any stage of a
divorce or separation. If you are newly separated,
you might find it useful to have guidelines that will
help you cope with your circumstances. You can use
the *Parenting Plan* as a framework for testing and
redefining your parenting arrangements during
separation. If you want the *Plan* to become a court
order, you may submit it to the court for its approval
as part of the temporary orders.

If you are getting a final divorce or legal separation, you will draft a *Plan* that will be submitted to
the court. Upon approval by the court, the *Plan* will
become part of your permanent orders or decree of
dissolution or legal separation.

You can create a *Parenting Plan* after your divorce or legal separation. If you have not preiously written a *Plan*, it may be helpful. You can also modify an existing *Plan*. If the modified or new *Plan* is submitted to the court, it will, upon approval, become an order of the court and will supersede any previous *Plans*.

Write your ***Parenting Plan*** at any stage of your divorce or separation. Then, review it periodically and modify it to meet your changed circumstances. If your ***Plan*** has been entered by the court as an order, you may need to submit your modification to the court for review and approval. In any event, use your ***Plan*** as a guide for the way in which you address the needs of your ***Post-Divorce Family***.

What Is the Best Time to Write a *Parenting Plan*?

If you want to design your *Post-Divorce Family*, it is better to start thinking about your *Plan* as early in the divorce process as possible. Put the family out in front, and put your anger and fear in a separate box—you can work on those issues individually.

The more you are able to segregate your anger and fear, define what your family wants and needs, and demand that you and the other parent consider the children and how much they will want to continue to love both of their parents, the better it will be for all of you. You will discover that getting through a divorce and coming out the other side is a process, and each family will do it at their own speed and in their own way.

It is difficult to work with a spouse or partner who suffers from mental illness, and it may be too dangerous to work alone with your spouse or partner if you or your children have been the victims of violence, abuse or neglect. This is a decision you must make. However, under most circumstances, if you insist on cooperation, create guidelines early in the process, and demand adherence to those guidelines, you might just save yourself a lot of time, money and stress.

What Else Should We Know about the Law?

The laws of your state will affect the way you approach your divorce or separation. Some of the provisions of your *Parenting Plan* involve only common sense and are aspirational. Others will have legal ramifications and are mandatory. Therefore, regardless of how you work out the terms of your *Parenting Plan*, you may want to obtain the opinion of a competent attorney to be certain that your solutions are consistent with your objectives and with the law.

> Your **Parenting Plan** will become an order of the court, so make sure your **Plan** says what you want it to say. Don't be vague or assume that the other parent "knew" what you meant. Spell it out clearly.

Anything Else? Yes! Remember the Five "Cs"

If you and the other parent agree to follow some basic guidelines, your parenting partnership will be more successful. Just remember the Five "Cs":

1. **Commit to Your Children**
   Consciously renew your commitment to your children. Place them first—on the top of your list of priorities. They must come before all else, including new relationships and *significant others*. In the midst of your divorce and the stress of life after divorce,

always remember: THE CHILDREN COME FIRST. This may seem obvious, but it is extremely difficult when the demands of single parenthood settle in on you.

This is a guideline for which there is no choice and no room for negotiation. If you follow this suggestion, you will give your *Post-Divorce Family* the greatest chance for success!

2. Compartmentalize Your Anger

For many people, divorce means conflict. Obviously, you and the other parent don't agree on certain things or you wouldn't be getting a divorce. But sometimes the conflict can turn into angry shouting matches, rage ... and worse. If it is played out in front of your children or where they can hear it, they will be affected, literally, for the rest of their lives.

Here's the challenge: compartmentalize your anger, your hurt, your fear, and your pain. Take those feelings and emotions away from the children, and do not allow the children to become observers of or participants in the conflict. This is difficult. But, it is terribly important.

3. Communicate with the Other Parent

You must find a way to effectively communicate with your former spouse or partner. Some people think this is ridiculous and say that if they could have communicated during their marriage, they wouldn't be getting a divorce. Maybe this is true. But—and it's a big but—the problem is that, as divorced parents, you *must* communicate.

Regardless of how you structure your decision-making, your parenting time, your dispute resolution procedure, or your financial arrangements, communication with the other parent is absolutely critical to your ability to raise the children successfully. Alternative ways of communication are discussed in Chapter 5.

4. Consider the Ideas of Your Children

For many years, professionals/experts have told parents that they should never discuss divorce matters with their children other than to tell the children that the divorce was not their fault. Now, we are listening to adult children of divorce who say that, while they didn't want the responsibility of actually making decisions and they didn't need to hear the intimate details of personal or financial problems, they desperately wanted their parents to listen to them, to consider their thoughts and opinions, and to incorporate their ideas into the fabric of their *Post-Divorce Family.*

Ideas for when and how to include your children in your *Parenting Plan* are discussed in Chapter 11, *Child-Inclusive Parenting Plans.*

5. Change Your Approach to Conflict

Be prepared. As you design and implement your *Parenting Plan*, you will probably find that certain issues will be easy to resolve and others will be more problematic. Likewise, problems may arise in the future that catch you off guard and beg for resolution.

To accommodate such occasions in a nonadversarial way, include a conflict resolution procedure in your *Parenting Plan*. These are discussed in Chapter 10 and will save you time, money and stress in the future. They may also serve as a deterrent and encourage joint problem-solving and cooperation.

Remember the 5 "Cs":
1. Children Come First—Always.
2. Compartmentalize Your Anger—
   Don't Scar Your Kids.
3. Communicate With the Other
   Parent—It's Imperative.
4. Consider the Ideas of Your Children—
   Listen to Them.
5. Change Your Approach to Conflict—
   Peaceful Dispute Resolution Saves
   Money, Time and Stress.

But What If ...?

What if you don't know how to prepare a *Parenting Plan* that is appropriate for your particular situation? How can you, for example, work with a former spouse or partner who is critical, angry or abusive? What problems will you emphasize? What issues can you ignore or play down? How can you provide for the inevitable changes that will occur as your children grow and your life's demands change?

Parenting Plans for Families After Divorce offers answers to these questions. You may use this book to identify issues and gain insight into parenting after divorce. You will be introduced to ideas that make parenting after divorce less stressful. And, you will explore ways to maintain a relationship with the other parent that work in the best interests of your children.

Good Luck!
The journey will be challenging,
but the destination—
raising strong and healthy children—
will be worth all the effort.

Chapter 2

The *Family Mission Statement*—
A Family Business Plan

What Is a *Family Mission Statement*?

The *Family Mission Statement* is one of the new tools you can use to define the way in which your family will function after the divorce. The *Mission Statement* recognizes that your family will still exist after the legal divorce is completed and answers questions like:

What are your dreams for your reconstructed family?

What are your values, purpose, and goals?

How will you divide the tasks to achieve the goals?

What are the obstacles that you must overcome to meet the goals?

How can you successfully work together?

The *Family Mission Statement* is very similar to a business plan that a company would create to be certain that all of the people who are involved in the business are moving together in a positive and productive way.

The *Family Mission Statement* is not required by state law to be included in your *Parenting Plan*. It is really an outline of the goals to which you aspire. Because many of the provisions of a *Parenting Plan* are mandatory and enforceable by the court, you may want to create a separate *Mission Statement* only for the use of your family and exclude it from the actual *Parenting Plan* that you submit to the court.

On the other hand, *Parenting Plans,* as a rule, contain many provisions that are aspirational and difficult to enforce, so whether you include it in your *Parenting Plan* is a decision that you should discuss and make with the other parent.

Will It Help Our Children?

We have learned from adults who experienced the divorce of their parents that, as children, they were hurt by their parent's inability to eliminate the divisive issues that permeated their lives. Some of the problems, such as living in two homes, are inevitable. However, some of the problems can be prevented or alleviated with a strong *Mission Statement* that clearly defines and reconciles differing values, approaches to parenting, ethics, and emotional support.

Many adult children of divorce look back on their parent's divorce with sorrow and resentment. Why? Nobody ever asked them for their ideas. They were excluded from all discussions of the divorce, and nobody seemed to care about their opinions.

Creating a *Family Mission Statement* is a wonderful way to address this problem. Children can become involved in designing their future without having to get involved in the adult issues of the divorce. The *Mission Statement* becomes proof that their parents were listening.

Creating a *Family Mission Statement* will require the cooperation of both parents and all of your children. Make it a fun experience.

Children need to know that they still have a family and that they can still count on the family for support. With their help and a little effort, you will produce an amazing tool that will send an overwhelmingly positive message of love and support to your children.

How Do We Write a
Family Mission Statement?

To write a *Family Mission Statement*, gather ideas from each family member. Ask each member to answer questions. For example, what is their idea of your family's purpose? What do they want their *Post-Divorce Family* to look like? What are their dreams? What is their vision? What results do they want to achieve? Then, sit down and talk. Compare ideas. Bring the ideas together, and start to write.

An example of a broad *Mission Statement* would be:

We, the Smith family, believe that our purpose is to maintain the dignity of each family member. We will help each member to grow personally, professionally, emotionally and spiritually. We will consistently focus on our family members and make decisions that are in their best interest. We will cooperate with each other, and we will be honest and loving. We are committed to academic excellence, community leadership, and financial success. We will each do our best to maintain a sense of humor, and we will listen to each person's ideas and opinions.

In contrast, your *Mission Statement* might be simple and direct:

> We will help each family member achieve success in their lives.

Or, you can define your values and then write specific tasks:

> We, the Jones Family, believe that our purpose is to empower each family member and support their individual and family goals. We agree that education, health, sports activities, religion, and financial survival are important to our family. To support these values in each home, we agree that:

- We will cooperate with the children's teachers and provide monthly assistance at their school.

- We will attend all parent-teacher conferences.

- We (the children) will complete all homework before we play or watch television.

- We will each serve nutritional meals in our homes.

- The children will contribute 20 percent of their allowance and financial gifts to their 529 Plans.

Write your *Family Mission Statement* in ink! Hang it on the wall where every family member can read it—often. Periodically review it. How are you doing? Does the *Mission Statement* need to be revised?

   Use it to measure your progress and to support your *Post-Divorce Family*.

Chapter 3

Decision Making—

No Waffling Allowed

What Is *Decision-Making?*

Even though you are divorced, you will need to define the way in which you will make decisions for your children. In this Chapter, you will find questions that will help you identify many of the decisions you must make. You may discover that you have already made some of them. There are others that you and the other parent may readily agree upon. And, there will be some that might be problematic for either or both of you.

The most significant decisions include health, education and general welfare. However, you may want to identify other issues that could present problems for you. Some parents, for example, want to clarify the children's religious upbringing. Some parents must protect their children from a spouse/ family member's substance abuse, involvement with pornographic material, or inappropriate behavior towards the children. The day-to-day decisions such as minor discipline matters, chores, allowance, curfew and hygiene generally will be made by the parent with whom the children are staying at any given time, but it is important that there be consistency from one house to the other.

> **As you go through this exercise, keep focusing on the children and identify the things that will help them the most. Listen to your children—they may want to share their concerns and give you some ideas. This is not a matter of which parent *wins* and which parent *loses*. You will want to create a *Post-Divorce Family* in which the children will be the winners. Place them first. Emphasize the strengths of your particular situation and correct the weaknesses.**

Health Decisions

You and the other parent might agree that your children need regular medical, dental and vision care and that, in an emergency, either of you may obtain reasonably necessary medical services for them. You might also agree (or your state law might require) that you can each have access to your children's records. But, other issues can present problems. When you discuss the health of your children, you will want to decide:

- The type of services that the children need or will need including medical, dental, optical, counseling, surgical or other.

- How you will choose the children's primary medical service providers and whether you will be limited to providers who are participants in your medical insurance plan.

- How you will meet the special medical needs, if any, of your children.

- Who will be responsible for selecting and paying for the children's medical insurance.

- How you will pay for uninsured medical expenses.

- How you will notify the other parent of problems a child may be having, particularly in the case of an emergency.

- Who will make medical appointments.

- Who will take the children to the appointments.

- Who will care for sick children.

- How you will exchange the children's prescription information and medication.

> Be sure to identify other medical issues that relate specifically to your children. The answers to your questions will become provisions in your **Parenting Plan**, if you so choose. If you run into a roadblock and cannot reach an agreement, you may want to review Chapter 10, *Disagreements—They Happen Too!*

Education Decisions

Few parents disagree about the importance of giving their children a good education. For many families, a divorce or separation will not change the way in which the children are educated. Other parents will need to reevaluate their educational choices because of changed circumstances. For example, you might have to move and choose a school that is close to your new home. Or, you might have to choose a public school rather than a private school because of the financial pressures of the divorce. When designing your *Parenting Plan*, you will want to decide:

- Where your children will attend school.

- How you will make decisions if a change of circumstances requires you to select a new school.

- How you will meet any special educational needs of your children.

- How each parent will participate in school activities.

- How school announcements, report cards and other information will be shared.

- Who will be identified on school records and notified in case of an emergency.

- Whether you will each have access to your children's records.

- Whether you want to include a provision regarding the choice and payment for postsecondary education.

> Like many issues, you will not be able to make all of the educational decisions at the time of your divorce or separation because you will not know your children's future needs. The best you can do is to design a process that describes how you will resolve unanticipated problems. This is where the suggestions presented in Chapters 9, *Change—It Happens* and 10, *Disagreements—They Happen Too!* will be helpful.

Religious Decisions

Parents rarely change their religious affiliation after divorce or separation. And, there's no issue when families have not participated in a formal religion and do not intend to raise their children in a specific religious denomination. Problems arise when parents are of different religions or one parent desires to involve the children in a new religion after the divorce or separation. Religious wars—even little ones—are destructive. From the decades of my mediation practice, here are the top concerns regarding religion:

- The choice, if any, of religion(s) for the children.

- How you will provide training in the chosen religion(s).

- How religious holidays will be celebrated.

- How you will plan and pay for expenses associated with religious ceremonies such as a First Communion or a Bar or Bat Mitzvah.

It may be your choice to select a primary religion for your children. Or, you might agree to take the children to the services and classes of your respective religions so they will have the benefit of learning about each parent's beliefs. You might also agree to ask the children to make the decision if they are mature enough to assume that responsibility.

One thing is clear. If religion becomes a battleground, you will violate the very tenets that you want to pass on to your children. Anger, hate and vengeance are not usually included in religious teachings, but these are the emotions that your children will witness (and learn) if you don't resolve this issue. Don't sabotage your principles in a religious war. Find a workable solution.

General Welfare Decisions

The decisions you will make under this section depend on your specific situation. It is a broad category, and you can include those decisions that you think will be important in the lives of your children. You will want to consider:

- How you will treat the other parent in the presence of the children.

- Whether you will attend counseling sessions with the other parent to learn how to separate the end of your intimate relationship and the beginning of your non-intimate parenting relationship.

- How you will communicate with the other parent and whether you will obtain professional help to teach you and the other parent how to effectively (and peacefully) communicate with each other about the children.

- Whether there will be rules regarding the way you entertain *significant others* in the presence of the children.

- Whether there will be step-parenting guidelines if either of you remarries or enters into a committed relationship.

- Whether there will be limits on the types of activities in which the children participate, and whether they may participate in activities that conflict with either parent's *Parenting Time*.

- Whether, if your child is biracial, you will help the child identify with one race or whether the child will participate and identify with both races.

- What will happen if one parent wants to move permanently with the children to a distant location.

- Whether your children need to be protected from the one parent or from certain family members or friends.

- Whether you will select a guardian for the children in the event of your deaths.

You may identify other issues that fall under the category of *general welfare*. Again, consider your children and place them above your desires.

If you and the other parent reach agreements on *Decision-Making* provisions, include them in your *Parenting Plan*. If you don't agree on certain issues, consider using some of the methods outlined in Chapter 10, *Disagreements—They Happen Too!*

Chapter 4

Parenting Time (Visitation)—

Making It Work for You and Your Children

How Will Our Children Spend Time with Each of Their Parents?

In your *Parenting Plan*, you will define a schedule that identifies when your children will spend time with each parent. You will want to consider the ages and developmental stages of your children and create a schedule that is appropriate for their needs. You will also want to consider your own needs as well as those of the other parent. In many cases, the children will want their parents to listen to their ideas and, at the very least, consider their preferences.

Laws generally provide that each parent has a duty to support his or her children, and, in some states, *Parenting Time* does affect the amount that is paid in child support. For example, the child support guidelines in your state may take the number of overnights that the children spend with each parent into consideration when determining the child support obligation.

It is unfortunate when the law creates a connection between money and *Parenting Time* because it can alter your decisions. What may be in the best interest of the children might be ignored because it affects the amount of money that is paid for child support. There are ways to resolve this problem, and they are presented in Chapter 8, *Finances—Sharing the Cost*.

> **Don't trade time with the children for money. Try to figure out the monthly, holiday and vacation *Parenting Time Schedule*s that are most appropriate for your children, for you, and for the other parent. Save the money issues for the Chapter 8 on *Finances—Sharing the Cost*.**

What Factors Should We Consider When Creating Our *Parenting Time Schedule*?

Before you actually choose a *Parenting Time Schedule*, consider how certain existing factors affect your decision. The *Schedule* will have a marked and long-term effect on your children. An appropriate *Schedule* will lessen the trauma and ease their problems. So, you will want to consider whether:

- Your children are too young to be away from either parent for extended lengths of time.

- Your children are old enough to spend overnights at each parent's home.

- Your children will spend extended amounts of alternating time with each parent or whether they should spend more time with one parent in order to have greater stability during, for example, the school week.

- You each have sufficient parenting skills and knowledge to adequately care for the children without the help of the other.

- You each can provide a physically safe environment for the children.

- You each can provide an emotionally safe environment for the children.

- You live close to the other parent or whether transportation will be a problem.

- You each can participate in your children's school and extracurricular activities.

- You need to make special arrangements to accommodate your schedule or the schedule of the other parent.

- Your children's relationship with their siblings or stepfamily members affects the *Parenting Time Schedule* that you design.

- You need to make special arrangements because you and the other parent are engaged in conflict that should be kept away from the children.

- There is concern that you or the other parent might harm the children or each other.

How Should We Deal with Special Problems?

Before you figure out what your *Parenting Time Schedule* will be, consider whether you need help to resolve the problems that you have identified. You might need to:

- Talk to your pediatrician, a child psychologist, your lawyer, your mediator or other professional to help determine a *Parenting Time Schedule* that is appropriate for your children. Many professionals are accustomed to helping people make these decisions—so don't hesitate to reach out and learn from their experience.

- Read. Take advantage of the many books and resources that are available on this subject. Some are suggested in Part Four of this book.

- Be honest about your ability to parent your children. During your marriage or relationship, you may have left much of the responsibility to the other parent. Now it is time for you to catch up. Don't hesitate to enroll in parenting classes or to hire a *parenting coach* who can observe your interaction with the children and make suggestions. You may want to get ideas from friends or from the other parent. Being a good parent requires that you have appropriate parenting skills. And, these certainly can be learned.

- Check out your place of residence. Is it safe for the children? Do you have adequate room for them to sleep? Can you help them arrange their rooms so they have a sense of belonging and ownership? Again, take suggestions. People will be more than happy to help. It can mean that your children feel welcome and protected.

- Acknowledge your physical or emotional limitations and those of the other parent, and structure the parenting time to accommodate problems. If one parent suffers from depression, for example, you may want to create a schedule that is flexible so the children can be with that parent during times when he or she is best able to cope with them. If one parent has a substance abuse problem that will affect the children, you will want to insist that no drugs or alcohol are used before or during the parenting time. You might need to create a *Parenting Time Schedule* that does not provide for overnights with one parent, or you might need to engage the services of a professional who will be

present during the parenting time and
supervise it.

- Consider using a nontraditional
  arrangement. Some parents adopt a *nesting*
  arrangement in which they each get a
  shared residence/apartment or separate
  residences/apartments. The children
  remain in the family home, and the parents
  move in and out of the family home
  during their respective *Parenting Time*.

  Alternatively, some parents remain in
  separate sections of the family home and
  design their *Parenting Time Schedule* just as
  they would if they were living in separate
  residences. Both of these "nontraditional"
  arrangements present challenges but, if
  carried out with respect and consideration
  of the other parent, can offer the children a
  positive alternative to moving back and
  forth between their parent's homes.

- Decide how you will transport the
  children from one home to the other (if
  you have separate residences) and to
  their activities. Parents often share this
  responsibility.

- Determine how, if either you or the other parent has irregular work schedules, you will decide on the *Parenting Time Schedule*. Sometimes, the best you can do is to maintain flexibility and agree on the schedule each week or each month. Try not to make it too hard on the children.

- Make special arrangements to accommodate the needs of children of different ages, and take your children's desires to be with step-siblings into consideration. This will make your *Parenting Time Schedule* more difficult to design—but it might, in the end, make life easier.

- Recognize if you are in a high conflict relationship with the other parent and must design a schedule by which you have little direct contact. Set up the exchange time, for example, so that the children are picked up from school rather than from the other parent's home. When the children are present, don't engage in conversation that you know will lead to a fight. Don't criticize or disparage the other parent in the presence of the children. Your children will thank you.

- Acknowledge that, if you are in fear of the children's' safety or of your own, you must talk to a lawyer. You must not jeopardize your safety or the children's safety to accommodate a *Parenting Time Schedule*.

  It is difficult for parents to confront potentially harmful situations. On the one hand, the children need to be with both parents. On the other hand, you do not want to place the children in an environment in which they could suffer physical or emotional damage. In the end, you must weigh the risks and benefits and choose a *Schedule* that protects the children.

Once you have identified the problems that you must address, you will be ready to design your *Parenting Time Schedule*. Read on!

How Do We Design a *Parenting Time Schedule*?

The easiest way to design a *Parenting Time Schedule* is to consider the monthly schedule first and then add the holiday and vacation schedules.

Monthly *Parenting Time Schedule*

It is helpful to work with a four-week schedule rather than a monthly schedule because it won't have to be altered by the varying number of weeks in a particular month. Try using the following format:

M	T	W	TH	F	S	S
M	T	W	TH	F	S	S
M	T	W	TH	F	S	S
M	T	W	TH	F	S	S

Begin by considering the factors that you reviewed in the preceding section. What are the ages of your children? Should they have daily contact with both parents? Are they old enough to begin overnights in two homes? Do they need to stay in one home during the week and share weekends with both parents? Are the children old enough and do they want to spend equal amounts of time with each parent? Do you need separate schedules for different aged children? Will transportation be a problem? Do you want to have a *nesting* arrangement in which the children stay in the family home, and the parents move back and forth into the home and maintain a separate residence or apartment? Do you intend to live in the same home after the divorce, and, if so, how will you share time with the children?

Next, use the above format by circling the over-nights with one parent. If you want to identify the overnights with each parent, use different colored markers to reflect time with Mom and time with Dad. Underline the days on which the children will spend afternoons or evenings with one parent. Look at the *Schedule*. Are there periods of time that are too long for the children to be away from one parent or the other? Does the *Schedule* meet your goals? Will the children be able to tolerate it? Have you identified the exchange times and the person who will be responsible for transportation?

There are many variations of monthly *Parenting Time Schedules*—so experiment. Keep drawing until you find one that suits each parent's needs and is in the best interest of your children. Remember, your ultimate choice should benefit the children. It is most likely that neither you nor the other parent will be fully satisfied, but, as in most of adult life, you will need to make accommodations in order to reach your goal. Your cooperation and ability to adapt will be a model for your children.

Holiday *Parenting Time Schedule*

Begin by identifying the holidays that are important to you. A typical list includes the following:

Thanksgiving	Easter
Christmas Eve	Chanukah
Christmas Day	Kwanzaa
New Year's Eve/ New Year's Day	Rosh Hashanah
Easter	Passover
3-Day Holidays including Presidents', Martin Luther King Jr., Labor Day, and Memorial Day	Fourth of July
Mother's Day and Mother's Birthday	Father's Day and Father's Birthday
Children's and Sibling's Birthdays	

Sometimes parents divide the holidays, and sometimes they alternate the holidays on a yearly basis. Vacations may also be considered at this point because you will have to accommodate the children's fall breaks, winter breaks, spring vacations or off-track schedules. Some parents make special provisions for these school breaks and others consider them in the vacation section below.

Vacation *Parenting Time Schedule*

If appropriate, you may stipulate that each parent may take the children for a vacation for a specified time each year. Some parents divide the school breaks and others merely state that they may each take the children for two week's vacation, for example, each year at a time to be mutually arranged. The length of the vacation time will depend on the ages of your children and their ability to be away from either parent for extended periods of time. You can include a provision that allows one parent the first choice of times in even-numbered years and the other the first choice of times in odd-numbered years.

This avoids possible conflict. You might also want to consider your time away from the children and include a provision that requires each parent to take the children for a period of time each year. This gives you a vacation from the cares of parenting.

Clarifying Your Expectations

Parents often include provisions that clarify expectations and prevent problems. Consider the following:

- **Child Care Option**
  If either parent must leave the children for a period of time, do you want a provision that the other parent will be given the first option to care for them?

- **Notification of Changes**
  Do you want to include a provision that identifies how you will communicate with the other parent if you need to change the schedule?

- **Special Requests**
  Will you make a good faith effort to accommodate the special requests of the other parent for attendance at, for example, weddings or family reunions? You can write that into your *Parenting Plan*.

- **Make-up Time**
  Some parents provide for ways to make-up missed *Parenting Time*. Others find that it is confusing to the children and conclude that they will not provide for make-up time. It really depends on your situation and your children's ability to cope with adjustments to the schedule.

- **Activities**
  Who will enroll the children in activities? What if the activities conflict with either parent's *Parenting Time*? Try to discuss

and agree on the children's schedules with the other parent so you won't run into problems. Don't schedule activities that occur during the other parent's *Parenting Time* without prior mutual agreement.

- **Modifying the *Schedule***
  Some parents set a certain time each year when they will review and modify the *Schedule*, if necessary. This can be particularly helpful if you must make plans to enroll the children in summer activities or you need to make advance travel plans.

- **Holidays and Vacations Supersede**
  Usually, the holiday and vacation *Parenting Time Schedules* supersede the monthly *Parenting Time Schedule*— except that neither parent may schedule a vacation during the other parent's holiday *Parenting Time*. Sound confusing? It can be. Just think of the holiday schedule and the vacation schedule as overlaying the monthly schedule.

- **Parental Responsibility**
  When does the *Parenting Time* begin and
  end and who is responsible for the
  children when they can't go to school due
  to illness, snow days, in-service days, etc?

- **Itinerary**
  If either parent leaves his or her
  residential state (or city) with the children,
  do you want to include a provision
  that the traveling parent will give the
  other an itinerary of the trip, including
  destinations, land line numbers if cell
  phones won't work, travel schedules and
  flight information. Will you include any
  restriction on international travel? Who
  will keep the children's passports? Will
  you need the other parent to sign a travel
  consent form?

- **Identification**
  Some parents agree to carry an
  identification card in their wallet or purse
  that lists the name and contact
  information for the other parent. There
  are instructions to contact the other
  parent in the event there is an incident or
  accident that affects the children.

If you are concerned about the safety of your children or can't trust the other parent, you may need to ask the court to design your *Parenting Time Schedule*. However, you can try to identify the most significant issues and see if you and the other parent can reach agreement on those issues. Think about compromising on the less important ones. It's not easy.

Things that Are Guaranteed to Make You Crazy!

Parents can design the most appropriate *Parenting Time Schedule* and, with a little effort, still make each other go berserk. To avoid problems and help the children, try to:

- Always be on time for the *Parenting Time* exchanges. Have the children ready. If you are delayed, call the other parent and "guestimate" your time of arrival or the time you will have the children ready.

- Send clean clothes with the children when they go back and forth.

- Send appropriate and nice clothes for the *Parenting Time.*

- Tell the other parent if you want the children to bring clothes for a special event.

- Let the other parent know in advance if the children will be spending time with your *significant other*. It's not fair to let the children break the news to the other parent.

- Avoid making disparaging remarks about the other parent (and this goes double for your family members and *significant other*). Do not allow the children to become participants in your problem.

- Let the children spend *real* time with you. They do not have to be entertained all the time. Give them chores. Read to them. Help them with their homework. By sharing the hard work, they will relate to you as a parent—not as a deep pocket.

- Tell the other parent about remarks the children make that cause you concern. It can help clarify problems, and, it will send a message to the children that their parents (both of them) are still in charge.

- Coordinate things such as bedtime and special diets in both homes.

- Go the extra mile. Be a good role model— even if no one thanks you for it. Your reward will be in knowing that you have given your best to the children.

There is no "one size fits all" perfect **Parenting Time Schedule**. Your **Post-Divorce Family** is unique. However, as a general rule, you will have fewer problems if you remember to treat the other parent and your children with respect and dignity. You will receive benefits that endure over time.

Chapter 5

Communication—

Yes, You Still Have to Communicate

Communicate with the Other Parent? Impossible!

Communication with the other parent can be difficult. And, no matter how much you may wish to avoid it, you will still have to talk to the parent of your children.

This is easy for many people. Others, however, will run screaming from the room at the mere mention of a conversation with the other parent. Why is it so hard?

Communication with anybody is complicated. It involves all of our senses (and some that haven't yet been discovered). When we communicate, we have to formulate an idea and tell that idea to another person. They must hear it, understand it, and respond to it. We then must hear, understand and respond to the answer. To make things more confusing, our spoken message is often layered with body language that sends messages which are inconsistent with what we have just said! Whew! Professionals spend a lifetime studying the process of communication.

But—add a divorce or separation to the mix including all the emotional stuff that goes with it, and you have a challenge. If you are trying to work with a person who has mental problems, physical problems or is limited by alcohol or drug abuse problems, communication is all but impossible.

If it's so complicated, why even try? You know the answer … because you have kids, and they need to have parents who can work together. Sorry about that.

So—How Do We Do It?

There are many ways to communicate about your children. Here are a few suggestions:

- Make an agreement (and stick with it) to limit your conversations to child-related issues and issues you have identified in your *Family Mission Statement*. Even though you may both be experiencing the pain of the divorce, you can't constantly rehash and blame. Talk only about what the kids need or want. Avoid discussions in front of the kids or within their earshot (and, incidentally, children can hear through walls—it's amazing).

54

- Choose a method by which you will communicate. Some people are able to speak in person or on the phone. Other people can't do this and prefer to send messages via fax, text, or email. You may also want to use a *real time* computer calendar such as the ones found on Google, or *www.OurFamilyWizard.com*, or *www.CoFamilies.com*. If you have an emergency involving your child or you need to make a last-minute schedule change, use the quickest method of communication—often the telephone.

- If you speak with each other by phone, be considerate. Limit the conversation. If the conversation becomes angry or off the subject, politely end the call, and then call back within 24 hours. If you need to leave a message, only leave one or two. If you receive a message, try to return the call promptly, especially if it involves a schedule change or a conversation with the children.

- If you text, email or fax, watch your language. Always let a message rest for a while before you send it. You'll discover that there are probably nicer ways to say things than you originally thought. Communicating by texting, email or fax will give you a record of the conversation, and that helps to keep people on a positive path.

- Follow a format for all forms of communication. First tell the other person that you are calling or emailing about a specific topic. Succinctly explain the problem or issue. Offer your proposed solution, and ask for a response.

- If you are the receiver, respond promptly either by (1) explaining your view of the problem or (2) telling the caller that you have to think about the call/email and you will return it within 24 hours. Then—keep your word. Return the call within 24 hours, and use your best efforts to find a solution to the problem.

- Try not to be accusatory or defensive. Before your children are raised and gone, you will confront at least one situation in which the child tells you an untrue story about the other parent or tells you only half the truth. You will need to confirm the information with the other parent. It's really hard to keep your head on straight when you receive or communicate unpleasant information. But—it's so important. Speak as though you are talking to a business partner—be polite and factual.

> **When you engage in safe and respectful communication, you send your child a message that he/she will not have to assume a parental role or carry messages. It gives your child the freedom to love each of you and enjoy childhood.**

Are There Other Resources We Can Use?

Yes. Often, couples need additional help in order to improve their communication skills. Here are a few suggestions:

- There are many professionals who are qualified to help you. Some of my clients

have attended basic and advanced
Parenting Classes that are conducted by a
mental health professional and focus on
communication. You can get referrals
from your attorney, your mediator, your
state Bar Association or from a family
law judge.

- You might try post-divorce counseling.
  Again, there are people who specialize
  in working with high conflict couples.
  This is not marriage counseling, and the
  focus is not on reconciliation. Rather,
  you will identify the things that are
  frustrating you and preventing you
  from communicating successfully—and,
  with the help of the counselor, try to
  correct them.

- Try mediation. In this form of dispute
  resolution, a neutral third party (the
  mediator) will facilitate the conversations
  between you and the other parent. The
  mediator will help you formulate a plan
  for communication or resolve other
  issues that are causing problems. If you
  agree, the mediator can draft a
  Memorandum that reflects your

agreement. You can, at your option, submit the Memorandum to the court to become an Order of the court. You can engage in mediation before or after your divorce.

> **Learning to communicate successfully will save you time and money. You will reduce hassles and have more time to enjoy your children.**

Chapter 6

Technology—

Get Online

Why Should We Worry about Technology?

When I was divorced in the 70s, we had a land line (with two extensions!) and one TV. No computers, no internet, no cell phones. If my kids needed to do research, I took them to the library. If they wanted to understand how a factory worked, we took a field trip.

In some ways, life is easier today. We can communicate with our children by cell phone and texting. They can research school reports, talk to their teachers, check in with their friends, and play interactive games on the Internet. Working parents can use Skype (voice and video calling) to touch base with their kids. We have an infinite variety of tools to find out where the children are and what they are doing.

But, in many ways, life has become more dangerous for children and more challenging for you as parents. Kids can step into disastrous situations that are light years beyond their experience and comprehension. This is why it's important to know what your children hear and see on the Internet, who they meet, and what they share about themselves online. The situation becomes extremely complex when you're divorced, your children live in two separate homes, and you and the other parent are not willing to establish and enforce similar rules and expectations in each home.

> **Worry about technology?—you bet! It is imperative for both parents to cooperatively design the rules that will apply in both of their homes. No wiggle room on this one. You must keep your children safe.**

Should We Include This Topic in Our *Parenting Plan*?

You can include any agreed upon provisions in your *Parenting Plan*. But—you don't want to create so many rules that you become overwhelmed. Try to find a balance that suits you and the other parent and meets the needs of your children.

What Are Some Guidelines that We Might Consider?

The following guidelines come from the many cases I have mediated and the problems that parents have had to resolve—after their kids have gotten into trouble. You can use a preventative approach and might consider including some or all of the following in your *Parenting Plan*:

- Keep the computers and TV's in a common area of your home. Don't let the kids have them in their bedrooms. There's too much temptation for children to get onto sites or watch shows that are inappropriate when no one is looking over their shoulder.

- Install safety devices/locks on all TV's and computers so you can monitor your children's online activities and prevent them from going to specific adult sites. You and the other parent should discuss and try to agree on the devices that you will use in each of your homes.

- Limit the time that your children spend on their video games. Identify the games that you and the other parent will buy. Discuss whether or not the children can take the games back and forth between your homes. Decide whether withholding the video games will be a form of discipline that each of you will use and whether this will be enforced in both homes.

- Talk to your children about potential online dangers and monitor their computer use. Explain the extensive reach of the Internet. Talk to them about social networking and the dangers of revealing personal information or pictures on sites like Facebook. Their profiles are not private and can be used by colleges and future employers to reject their applications. It's easy for a predator to create a profile, pretend to be a child, and lure kids into inappropriate relationships. Help your children use the Internet safely and make sure that your efforts are duplicated by the other parent in his or her home.

- Keep all porn sites off your computer. Dump the pornographic videos (if you have them). Lock your computer, and don't let your children have access to sites that are age inappropriate. Obviously, don't watch adult movies while your kids are staying with you. Remember, they can see and hear through walls!

- If you want to include a provision in your *Parenting Plan*, you might consider the following:

> We agree to jointly define and establish boundaries for each child's use of social media, such as Facebook, Twitter and texting. We shall establish guidelines for parental monitoring of each child's use of Facebook or any other social networking website and shall discuss any concerns we have regarding such use; we shall jointly agree on the consequences for the misuse thereof. We shall establish guidelines for monitoring the text messages that the children send or receive. We shall discuss any concerns we have regarding such text messaging, and

we shall jointly agree on the consequences for the misuse thereof. We shall each maintain computer filters/parental controls on all applicable electronic devices in our respective homes to prevent our child's access to inappropriate Internet content.

> **You must communicate with the other parent. If you run into problems or if the children are abusing their privileges at either home, discuss the problem and jointly choose a solution. Support each other! Your child's life may depend on it.**

Chapter 7

Nontraditional and Special Needs Families—

Practical Considerations

In the 1950s and 1960s, the typical American family was thought by many to be made up of a mother, a father, a couple of kids and, of course, a dog. In the iconic television show, *Leave it to Beaver*, the family was portrayed as Anglo with two happily married parents—June and Ward Cleaver—and two cute (and well-behaved) children, Theodore ("Beaver") and Wally. The Cleaver family was held out to be the ideal suburban family in the mid-twentieth century.

Today, we recognize numerous combinations of nontraditional and special needs families and the unique and complicated issues they have. Basically, the suggestions in *Parenting Plans For Families After Divorce* apply to nontraditional/special needs families. However, because these families face additional challenges that courts have neither the time nor the resources to resolve, it is extremely important for the parents to work together and design a *Parenting Plan* that accommodates their particular needs.

Within this chapter, some types of nontraditional/ special needs families are identified. Included are suggestions for issues that often demand consideration. It is by no means exhaustive but hopefully will send you down a path of further exploration.

Families with Special Needs Children

Special needs children have or are at increased risk to develop chronic physical, developmental, behavioral, or emotional problems. They often require special health and other services. In addition to the provisions that have been previously discussed in this book, parents of special needs children must consider:

- Whether your child needs special therapy, medication, equipment, and treatments and how they will be provided.

- Whether your child might harm himself or others and how that situation will be handled.

- Whether parenting time in two homes is appropriate and whether you are each able to provide and care for the physical and emotional needs of your child.

- How the demands of your child's care will impact your ability and the ability of the other parent to maintain individual lives and careers. Will you share the requirements of your child's care with the other parent, including child care and attendance at appointments?

- How you will both interact with the child's teachers, physicians, and therapists. Determine how you will make decisions about the child's care.

- How you will maintain your child's records.

- Whether there are special programs in which your child should be enrolled. How will you choose the programs and who will pay for them?

- How you will communicate with the other parent.

- How you and the other parent will
  arrange for time away from your
  child (you will need vacations).

- How you will work with your other
  children to be sure that they receive
  the attention and love that they
  deserve.

The considerations that are presented in this
section barely scratch the surface of the issues with
which parents of special needs children are confronted. If you would like additional information, you
may wish to read *The Special Needs Child and Divorce*
by Margaret "Pegi" S. Price. It is published by the
American Bar Association and presents a guide for
evaluating and handling special needs cases.

Gay, Lesbian, Bisexual, and Transgender ("GLBT") Parents

Many GLBT parents have children from previous
opposite sex marriages or relationships, and many
GLBT individuals and same-sex couples are having
children by means of artificial insemination, in vitro
fertilization, surrogacy and adoption. If you are
married or have a legal relationship with your child
(such as a co-parent or second-parent adoption), the

dissolution of your relationship will be similar to the divorce process for opposite-sex parents. However, if you do not have a legal relationship with the other parent or with your children, you will face certain hurdles because the law provides little, if any, guidance. Therefore, in addition to the other suggestions in this book, you may want to consider:

- How you will legally provide for your child. You and the other parent will need to design your own *Parenting Plan*. Mediation and sound legal advice are important in such situations.

- How you and the other parent will help your child understand the changes in your family. If a child is born to or adopted by GLBT parents, it is likely that the child will have had contact with both gay and straight communities. It is more difficult for a child who has grown up thinking that his parents were straight and one parent "comes out."

  This situation is not uncommon but must be approached with great care and perhaps the help of a counselor. It's a situation in which the child's needs must be considered first. Let your child go at his own speed, and, as hard as it is, resist sharing every aspect of your new world with him until he is ready.

- How you, as parents, will provide a financial safety net for your child. In situations where no specific law applies, many GLBT parents have enormous problems. Under the divorce laws, financial guidelines for parents and children are clearly defined.

  If there is no law, there is no obligation to pay maintenance/alimony, and this can place one parent in a perilous financial situation. How will you handle this? What are your expectations and those of the other parent? What will your family design be?

- What your rights are if you are not on your child's birth certificate? If both parents are on your child's birth certificate, you may have the same rights and responsibilities as opposite-sex partners. If only one parent is on the birth certificate, you will want to review the laws of your state to clarify your legal position.

We can argue endlessly about the failure of our laws to provide for a significant segment of our community. Regardless of this inadequacy, we still have children who need their families. Hopefully, you will seize the opportunity to create a positive result for your children. For more information, you may want to read, *Ordinary Issues—Extraordinary Solution: A Legal Guide for the Colorado GLBT Community*, by Kimberly R. Willoughby and published by Bradford Publishing Company.

Never Married Parents

The issues faced by parents who have never been married are greatly influenced by the length and quality of their relationship before they have a child. If you have had a long-term successful relationship with the other parent, and you support each other and your child, your issues will not be significantly different from married parents.

However, if you only knew the other parent for a very short period of time, your situation will be more problematic because you will be raising your child with a relative stranger. In such a situation, it will be important to learn about the other parent and to find common ground on which you can create a family for your child. Please consider:

- How you will get acquainted. If you are going to be co-parents, you will want to know about each other's values, likes, dislikes, education, family history, health history, employment history, addictions and the like.

  You will want to know about the other parent's family members, especially if they are going to have contact with your child. Meet the other parent's family members and, if possible, establish a relationship with them.

  If you can't do this on your own, think about working on it in mediation. You can use the neutral mediator to facilitate communication and help you learn things that will be very important to you and your child. Your family members and the other parent's family members may participate, if you all agree.

- How you will design the way in which you function as a family. It's often difficult to balance all of the interests that are involved in this type of relationship.

You may be able to use the suggestions in Chapter 2, *The Family Mission Statement— A Family Business Plan* to help you draft a *Family Mission Statement.* If your situation is one that is safe for you and your child, it will benefit your child to have a high-quality relationship with both parents.

- How you and the other parent will learn parenting and co-parenting skills. Don't be shy about talking to friends and family. They can give you the benefit of their experience. Research the support services that are available in your community. This would include co-parent education classes, employment and housing assistance, and child support enforcement agencies (if that is an issue for you).

   You may want to consider hiring a parenting coach who can give you "hands on" assistance with your parenting. You will have to search out these resources. They are often offered at community centers or associated with court systems.

- How you will define your legal relationship. Just like married parents, you will want to agree on how you will make major decisions for your child, how your child will spend time with each of you and how you will share the financial responsibilities for your child. You will also want to protect yourself and your child if the other parent becomes disabled, ill or dies.

Again, using the mediation process to find answers to touchy questions can be very helpful for unmarried parents. If you reach agreement, it should be submitted to the court to become an order of the court. If you don't reach agreement, you will want to go to court to secure your rights and your child's rights.

- The importance of making a commitment to treat each other and your child with respect and cooperation. Your child will have a better chance to be successful.

Multiracial/Multicultural Parents

The number of multiracial/multicultural children has increased in the United States due to interracial marriages/relationships and international adoptions. However, even though the numbers have increased, these kids still face challenges, and parents of multi-racial/multicultural children may want to consider:

- How you will define and support your child's racial/cultural identity. Will you choose to support a multicultural life for the whole family? Will you support immersion in the language, traditions, and customs of all family members? Or, will you take a more defined approach and support only one race or culture? Will your child have a voice in this decision? Your agreement with the other parent on this issue will make your child's life much easier.

- How you will teach your child to cope with discrimination and societal biases. You will want to work with the other parent to encourage your child to communicate openly with both of you regarding any problems. You will want to develop a means of sharing that information and jointly deciding on any action you want to take.

- How you will establish support networks for your child with grandparents, relatives, neighbors, school and the greater community. As parents of a multiracial/multicultural child, the necessity of support networks may seem more apparent to you than it is to other parents. However, in a divorce situation, it is something that you may want to specifically discuss and agree upon.

• How you will deal with the issue of child abduction—if that is a concern for you.

Non-Parents as Parents

Non-parents are people who step in to raise a child when one or both of the biological parents has died or is unable to care for the child due to poverty, divorce, addiction, child abuse/neglect, mental or physical illness, or incarceration. Non-parents may be the child's grandparents, foster parents, or other relatives. Often, non-parents assume responsibility at their own financial and emotional expense in order to provide love and care for a child who desperately needs them.

Problems arise when the biological parent returns and wants to resume the role of the parent to the exclusion of the non-parent. The situation is similar to a divorce and is fraught with legal problems. If the case goes to court, the biological parent may be found to have superior rights to the non-parent if the biological parent can demonstrate that he/she is a fit parent, and it is in the child's best interest to be with him/her. Therefore, if you are a non-parent, you will want to:

- Carefully design your legal and emotional relationship with the biological parent(s). Consult a lawyer and come to a written agreement, if possible.

- Research outreach services and benefits currently available. If you are a grandparent, check with the American Association of Retired Persons Grandparent Information Center for help.

- Try to maintain an amicable relationship with the biological parent(s).

- Be prepared for challenges and change.

- Don't be deterred. Your help is priceless.

Children and parents in nontraditional/ special needs families experience problems that can be very complex. In some cases, there is little or no law to guide important family decisions. In other cases, judges do not have the time, expertise, or resources to give appropriate consideration to many of the issues that must be resolved.

It is often better for the parents to sit quietly with each other and, if necessary, their attorneys, counselor or mediator, and design a *Parenting Plan* that addresses the needs of each family member.

Chapter 8

Finances—

Sharing the Cost

Laws in all states provide for the financial support of children of divorce. Each state has a different formula or way of calculating child support, and it is important to know the law that applies to you.

But, here's the reality: children are expensive, and regardless of the way in which you calculate child support in your state, you as a parent, have a duty to provide for them.

Be realistic about the needs of your children rather than focusing on how much money you will pay or receive. Think about the expenses that the children will incur; how you will share those expenses with the other parent, whether they should be included in the calculation of child support, and how you will pay for your share. Money is an emotional issue as well as a practical one. Advance planning will help smooth the stressful times.

Things to Consider

- **Extraordinary Medical Expenses**

  How will you share and pay for the children's uninsured medical expenses? The law in your state may mandate a solution. In Colorado, for example, the parent receiving child support generally pays for uninsured expenses under $250 per year per child. Anything that costs more than that is shared in proportion to incomes. However, if the children spend substantial amounts of time with each parent or if your situation presents other factors that would make this division unfair, you can agree to share all uninsured expenses in a specific proportion.

- **Life Insurance**

  The length of time during which child support is paid is defined by statute. Generally, it lasts until a child becomes 18 or 19. If you die during that time, your obligation for child support does not die with you. Each parent should maintain life insurance (or other benefits) for the children so the surviving parent will not

82

have to take on the total financial responsibility for them. Many parents create a will and a trust and name the children as beneficiaries in trust. Some parents name the other as the direct beneficiary if they believe that they will spend the insurance proceeds for the benefit of the children. You might also design a procedure to verify that the life insurance policy is, at any given time, in effect and the beneficiaries have not been changed.

- **Extracurricular Activities**
  Minor extracurricular activities will probably be paid for from child support. But, if you anticipate that your children will participate in competitive sports, sleep away camps, tutoring, or the like, you need to decide if you can each afford your child's participation and how you will pay for it. Be sure to adequately communicate your thoughts to the other parent. If you try to commit the other parent's money (or time) without prior agreement, you will end up with friction that can erupt into major problems.

- **Automobiles and Insurance**
  They're expensive. Discuss what you
  will pay (if anything) and what the child
  must provide.

- **Religious Training and Ceremonies**
  Payment for expensive religious training
  and ceremonies such as a Bar and Bat
  Mitzvah or a wedding can be included
  in your *Plan*. Anticipate these expenses, if
  appropriate.

- **Extraordinary Clothing Expenses**
  As children get older, or if they
  participate in activities that require
  special clothing, their expenses will
  increase. You might want to consider
  sharing expenses such as winter clothes,
  prom dresses, or sports clothing. Child
  support covers the basics, but it can be
  inadequate for older children. If money
  is tight, you might have to limit expenses
  or ask the children to contribute.

- **Transportation**
  If the children must travel great distances
  to be with the other parent, you will want

to discuss how the transportation expenses will be paid. As part of the child support calculation, most parents share the cost of each ticket in proportion to their incomes. In other cases, one parent pays for the entire expense.

- **Private School Tuition**
  Is private school an option or a necessity for you? If so, you must figure out how to pay for it. It's better to do that before the child enrolls!

- **Postsecondary Education Expenses**
  In many states, courts do not have the authority to order parties to pay for their children's postsecondary education expenses. You can agree to share these expenses and figure out a savings program to meet your goals if that is appropriate for your situation.

Things that Are Guaranteed to Make You Crazy!

There are few things that make people angrier or more desperate than not having enough money. Even when money is tight, you will want to:

- Always make sure that child support is paid on time.

- Always make sure that your child's educational and special events fees are paid on time. If you have problems, such as a job loss, discuss it with the other parent. Don't ignore the problem.

- Acknowledge that you each have a duty to support your children, and make sure that happens.

- Acknowledge the contributions of the other parent. It doesn't cost any money to say, "thank you."

- Spend child support for the children. If you have questions about how the child support is spent by the receiving parent, discuss it before it becomes a problem.

- Avoid discussing the financial arrangements with the children. If there is a problem, talk about it with the other parent—not with your children.

Money problems are challenging, but you know that kids are expensive, and you know that two households cost more than one. So, work with the other parent to stretch your *Post-Divorce Family* dollars and make finances less of an issue. It's difficult, but possible.

Chapter 9

Change—

It Happens

What Happens if We Need to Change Our *Plan*?

The only guarantee in life is that things will change. A *Parenting Time Schedule* that works well for a one-year old will be inappropriate for a teenager. A *Parenting Plan* that works well when you live in close proximity to the other parent won't be adequate if one of you moves to another city. You might also find that the roles and responsibilities you were willing to assume immediately after the divorce or separation will not work when you become employed or remarried. It is easier if you anticipate change, maintain flexibility and react to it in a positive way that is helpful to the children.

You can always modify your *Plan* (and your *Family Mission Statement*) by mutual agreement, and many changes can be made informally. Some changes will have legal ramifications, however, and you will want to submit an amended *Plan* to the court and ask that it become an enforceable court order.

What Should We Anticipate?

- **Conflict**

  There are many reasons for the conflict that occurs between parents, but, what should you do about it? You can get counseling if the problem is yours. You can attend communication counseling, parenting classes, or therapy with the other parent so you can jointly address the issue that is causing the problem. Or, you can follow the *Dispute Resolution* process that you design in your *Parenting Plan*. If nothing works, you may have to restructure your interaction with the other parent and modify your *Parenting Plan*.

- **Crises**

  Crises are inevitable, and you might try to anticipate how, as parents living separately, you will react to them. Ideally, you should each be able to contact the other parent if there is an emergency. You might also want to be certain that you each have the phone numbers of physicians, family members and other professionals with whom your children are involved. Expect the best, but plan a neutral and pragmatic way to deal with problems.

- **Children's Needs**
  As children grow, their needs will change. Anticipate that you will have to adjust the *Parenting Time Schedule*. Anticipate that there will be greater demands on both of you as the children become more involved in activities. Anticipate that it costs more money to raise older children. Be willing to review your *Parenting Plan* (and *Family Mission Statement)* on a regular basis and adjust it to accommodate the children's changing needs.

- **Parental Needs**
  Parents have needs too! Your life will inevitably change, and those changes may affect the way in which you are able to parent your children. It is much easier to jointly acknowledge new directions and revise the *Plan*, if necessary.

You can always modify your *Parenting Plan* informally—and that works well for many parents. But, some parents need to clarify their expectations in writing and submit them to the court to become an order of the court. This leaves less room for later misunderstandings, and the order can be enforced by the court.

Chapter 10

Disagreements—

They Happen Too!

Get Ready—Disputes Happen!

At the time of your divorce or separation, it is impossible to identify all of the child-related problems that will confront you in the future. Even if you could, you and the other parent will not agree 100 percent of the time. For some issues, you will reach an easy compromise. For other issues, you might want to give one parent the final decision-making authority. And, for many issues, you might want to consider structuring a dispute resolution process that enables you to resolve problems.

If you can't agree, you can always ask a judge to make a decision for you because the court will have continuing jurisdiction over your children. This is the least desirable option because you're giving your parental authority to a third person who doesn't know the children. However, sometimes it's necessary, and it's those times that make us inordinately appreciative of a responsive and knowledgeable judiciary.

What Are Some Peaceful *Dispute Resolution* Techniques?

When you do not agree, consider using some of the following processes and write them into your *Parenting Plan*:

- **Negotiation**
  Negotiation is the least intrusive method of dispute resolution. This is a process in which you discuss the problem directly with the other parent and try to find options that work for each of you. You may want to have your lawyer or other advisor involved if you need some help.

- **Mediation**
  If you can't negotiate directly with the other parent, you can include a mediation provision in your *Parenting Plan*. In mediation, you hire a neutral third party (the mediator) to facilitate your discussion and help you find an answer that is acceptable to both of you. The mediator has no decision-making authority; the agreement that you reach is

yours. You will control the structure of
the mediation. Attorneys or other
specialists such as counselors or financial
consultants may be present at the
mediation if you so choose.

New mediation models that include
the children are identified in Chapter 11.
They provide amazingly effective forums
in which children can safely and
appropriately express their ideas.

Whether you mediate only with the
other parent or whether you design a
model in which you include the children,
you will find that mediation is a
remarkable process for resolving
disputes. It is private and confidential. It
is less expensive than going to court. It
can be easily scheduled, and you may
find it to be very empowering. Like every
form of dispute resolution, however,
mediation does have some risks, and
these should be discussed with your
lawyer and/or the mediator.

- **Collaborative Law**
This is a form of alternative dispute
resolution in which you and the other
party each retain collaboratively-trained

attorneys and other specialists such as a divorce coach, a mediator, or a financial specialist, who will help you work through the issues of your case and reach resolution without going to court.

- **Arbitration**

  In arbitration, you hire a neutral third party (the arbitrator) to actually decide your case. It is similar to a court hearing but is usually less formal. The arbitrator acts as a judge and will make a decision that will be binding unless you otherwise agree in advance. Arbitration provides very limited rights of review.

  Sometimes, people try mediation first. If there are issues for which no agreement has been reached, the mediator (or another agreed upon third party) acts as an arbitrator and makes a final decision. This process is called *Med-Arb*.

- **Litigation**

  If you have obtained a divorce or separation from the court, that court will have continuing jurisdiction or authority to hear matters involving your children. If you can't solve a problem; if you want

to identify a date on which an action,
such as modification of child support,
would be effective; or if you need
immediate help, you can file a motion
with the court and ask the judge to make
a decision.

- **Outside Experts**
  Another way to solve problems is to ask
  the court to appoint or agree to use
  experts. You may need the help of a
  professional evaluator, a Special Master,
  a legal representative for the child, a
  decision-maker, a parenting coordinator,
  a child/family investigator, a guardian
  ad litem, or a special advocate to help
  you. If such experts are recognized in
  your state, their authority will be defined
  by statute.

**The more you are able to use peaceful
Dispute Resolution methods to resolve
problems, the more time, stress and
money you will save. The benefits are
directly proportional to the investment!**

PART TWO

Listening to Your Children

Chapter 11

Child-Inclusive Parenting Plans—

Are You Listening?

What Is a *Child-Inclusive Parenting Plan*?

A *Child-Inclusive Parenting Plan* is one that incorporates your children's ideas and preferences. It is a way to acknowledge your children and include them in the formation of your *Post-Divorce Family*. Children usually want to speak—especially older children. But, even younger children have good ideas about things that affect their lives. We need to listen to them.

This idea of giving children a *voice* in the divorce process is relatively new. For many years, divorce professionals relied on a principle that has stood as one of the few bright lines in family law—never involve the children in divorce issues.

However, we now understand what seems rather obvious. Children are part of the family and are participants in family transitions. They are stakeholders and have a significant interest in the success of their family. They may not want to be responsible for actually making decisions and they may not want to know all of the ugly details of the divorce, but they do want to be heard on major issues that affect them and the family. They want their parents to listen or they may want to speak to a third party who will communicate their ideas to their parents.

> When it comes to issues that directly affect them, children want to know that they are part of the solution, and a *Child-Inclusive Parenting Plan* will help you make that happen.

Should Children's Ideas Always Be Included in the *Parenting Plan*?

No. There are certain issues that you and the other parent will decide regardless of the children's opinions. That's part of parenting. But, there are many issues and situations that beg for collaboration between you and your children, and this can be accomplished directly or through a third party such as a counselor or mediator. Whether you ultimately include the children's ideas in your *Plan* will be up to you and the other parent or the court.

As parents, unless you have unusual circumstances, you will retain authority over all matters involving your children. You may want your kid's input on some things and not on others. For example, safety issues are generally nonnegotiable. You do not need to debate your child's participation in high risk activities, choice of friends, use of the Internet, and use of drugs and alcohol. You might want to listen to their opinions on these issues, but you as a parent have the responsibility to keep your children safe.

There are other decisions that cry out for your children's participation. And, they *will* participate—either verbally or by their behavior. For example, you and/or the other parent will choose their doctors. If your kids hate the person you choose, you'll have a difficult time getting them to appointments. While you have the ultimate authority to choose the doctor, it is better to find one that meets your standards and relates well to your child. It saves a lot of hassle if you respect and listen to your child's opinion. It also sends a message to your child that you care. This is enormously significant.

Another area in which kids can participate is the design of the *Parenting Time Schedule* (visitation). It's very difficult for children to travel back and forth between their parent's homes. It takes time, effort and enormous concentration at a point in their lives when you are asking them to do well in school, make friends, participate in extracurricular activities, and generally be good kids. They will want to help you design a schedule that takes their needs into consideration.

You and/or the other parent will be responsible for the ultimate decisions you make for your children. However, they may have ideas that will make their lives easier—such as how many consecutive overnights they spend with either parent or how they would prefer to spend Spring Break. They will want you to take their school and activity schedules into consideration. There are many other things that you must accommodate, and you may not be able to create a schedule that totally meets each child's expectations. But—if your children are allowed to speak to these issues, they will know that you have heard them and validated their effort.

What Factors Should We Consider Before We Try to Include Our Children?

As you might have guessed, there is no one rule that applies to all families. The success of creating a *Child-Inclusive Parenting Plan* depends on factors that vary from family to family. Therefore, before starting, consider the following:

- Are you and the other parent relatively free from emotional or mental health problems?

- Are you and the other parent free from addictions (drugs or alcohol, for example)?

- Are you and the other parent willing to work together for the benefit of the children?

- Have you and the other parent been able to maintain a relatively low-conflict relationship?

- Are you and the other parent able to communicate about issues regarding the children?

- Are you and the other parent willing and able to follow through on commitments you make to your children?

- Are your children physically and emotionally safe with both you and the other parent?

- Can you and the other parent agree not to chastise or ridicule your children when they express their ideas?

- If your child expresses his opinions to a third party, such as a counselor, are you willing to respect the confidentiality of that conversation and not ask your child to reveal the information that he gave to that person?

- If you and the other parent make a promise to your child, are you each willing and able to keep it, to the best of your ability?

- Are you willing to do your best to work with the other parent to create a happy and successful childhood for your child?

- Are you willing to help your children understand that their ideas are important, but it is you, the parents, who will make the final decisions?

- Do your children want to talk to you about the divorce?

- If you and the other parent were able to answer, "Yes," to these questions, then you are prime candidates for

creating a *Child-Inclusive Parenting Plan*.
Congratulations!

Is There More than One Way to Include the Children in Our *Plan*?

Yes! There are many different child-inclusive models
that can be used. You will select a model that best
fits your needs and the needs of your children. Each
model provides ways in which a child's needs can
be expressed and considered in divorce without
compromising the safety of the child or the integrity
of the legal process. You might choose one of the
following:

- **Family Mediation**
  In the family mediation model, you, the
  other parent and your children meet in
  mediation with the mediator to discuss
  relevant issues such as *Parenting Time
  Schedules*. It's a great time to create a
  Family Mission Statement and jointly set
  goals and objectives for your *Post-Divorce
  Family*. Meeting together with your
  children can be difficult. It is important to
  leave your anger at the door and focus on
  the best interests of your children. The
  mediator will facilitate the meeting and

help each of you develop ideas and plan for your future.

- **Evaluative Mediation**
  In evaluative mediation, you retain a trained mental health professional to act as a mediator. You will be asked to complete a detailed questionnaire and work with the mediator to examine and resolve family disputes. The process can take ten to fifteen hours. Children may be included as the parties and the mediator deem appropriate.

- **Mediator Interviews with the Children**
  In this model, the mediator interviews your children outside of the mediation setting. Both lawyer mediators and mental health mediators are able to perform this service. Before the mediator meets with the children, the mediator obtains a written consent to the interview from you as well as a confidentiality agreement that provides that the interview with the children will be confidential. Additionally, you are asked to agree (and the children are so informed) that the mediator will discuss

only those issues with you that have been previously approved by the children. The mediator meets with the children to discuss their concerns and ideas regarding your divorce. The children identify the information they want the mediator to share with you, and the remainder of their conversation is confidential.

The mediator subsequently conducts a mediation session with you and the other parent and will discuss the concerns the children have identified and given permission to share. Ideally, you will incorporate some or all of the children's suggestions in your initial or modified *Parenting Plan*. It is a good idea to have the mediator conduct a follow-up interview with the children.

- **Child Specialist Interviews with the Children**
  With this model, a child specialist is chosen by the parties (or by the court) to interview the children and bring their concerns to the parents in the mediation sessions. The child specialist is an individual who, by their education and

training, is competent to work with the children. The child specialist uses similar guidelines as the mediator who interviews the children. This model is widely used in Australia and New Zealand. It has been successful in creating durable agreements between the parents and reducing the initiation of new litigation.

- **Judicial Interviews with the Children**
  Studies show that some children, particularly older children in contested cases, appreciate the opportunity to talk to the judge. There is an increasing awareness of the importance of having the ultimate decision maker hear the children's ideas. The children often want the judge to know that his or her decision will have a profound effect on their lives. They believe that the judge can make a better decision if he or she has first-hand information. Children sometimes prefer to have their discussion be confidential so they will not hurt their parent's feelings.

  Judicial interviews place the judge in a difficult position if he or she rules against the wishes of the child. Some judges may even want to talk to the child after the ruling is issued to help the child understand the decision. The children's conversation may not be confidential if, by law, it must become part of the record.

- **Therapeutic Intervention with Children**
  In some cases, it is helpful for the children to work with a therapist or counselor to discuss their opinions. In appropriate cases and with the children's consent and participation, the therapist meets with the parents and the children to facilitate discussion of concerns, expectations, and goals.

  This method requires a written consent from the parents, a confidentiality agreement, and the creation of a privileged relationship beween the children and therapist. Therapeutic intervention is a very successful method in cases where children want to confront one or both parents but need the help of the counselor to facilitate that communication.

- **Child's Legal Representative**
  Children can have lawyers too, and the lawyers often serve a very useful

purpose. They can attend mediation with the child and present or support the child's ideas and concerns. They can represent them in court if the matter must go before a judge. And, they can act as a spokesman for the child and provide a way by which the child's voice can be expressed to and heard by the parents. Expensive? Yes. Worth it? Yes, in many cases.

How Should We Prepare the Children to Participate in the Process?

If you are considering using one of the child-inclusive models, it is likely that your children have already indicated their desire to be heard. You are just providing a forum so that can happen in a constructive way. Even so, there are things you can do to prepare kids for their participation:

- Ask them to write down their ideas. Ask them to identify the issues that they would like to discuss with the counselor/mediator/child specialist/ judge ("third party"). Tell them that they do not have to share their ideas with you unless they choose to do that.

- Regardless of the model you choose, tell the children that their meeting will be confidential and that the third party will report only those things that are requested to be reported by your child.

- Tell them that you and the other parent have agreed that you will not question them about the contents of their meeting with the third party and that they have no obligation to share that information with you unless they want to do that.

- Reassure them that they can have a follow-up meeting with the third party, if they wish.

- Prepare them for the fact that some things aren't fixable and that, while you will try very hard to accommodate their requests, you are the parents and you will make the final decision.

It would be wonderful if you could grant every wish that the child might have— but you can't. It is most important, however, that your child knows that you, as parents, will jointly discuss and take his concerns into consideration. That's the important part. You're working together to make your child's life better.

We're Still Not Sure ...

There is no legal requirement that you have to include your children's ideas in your *Parenting Plan*. Divorce professionals and participants, including parents, lawyers, mental health professionals, and judges recognize that children's involvement in the parent's divorce is complicated. However, before you go to court, think about whether one of the models described in this Chapter would be helpful in your particular situation. These models offer methods for including children's ideas and enabling parties to reach positive solutions without giving children undue authority or responsibility. They can produce lasting results and avoid the more costly alternative of using a court-appointed representative such as a Guardian *ad litem*, a Child Family Investigator, or a Parental Responsibilities Evaluator.

Every divorce is different and requires the application of appropriate methods of resolution. Some cases do not lend themselves to the use of any child-inclusive models, but all cases involving children should be individually reviewed and evaluated to see if the use of a child-inclusive model would be beneficial.

PART THREE

Making Your
Parenting Plan Work

Chapter 12

Guaranteeing Failure— Guaranteeing Success

What Are the Worst Things that You Can Do to Your Children (and Guarantee Failure in the Process)?

There are things you can do that will sabotage the best of *Parenting Plans*, and there are other actions you can take that practically guarantee success.

I'm a list maker. In my 30 years of working with families in divorce and mediation, I've identified the four worst things that you can do to your children (and guarantee that your *Parenting Plan* will fail). You will damage your children (sometimes irreparably) if you engage in:

- **Ongoing Conflict**
  Children can survive divorce. What hurts them is ongoing conflict between their parents. It makes them feel insecure— they can never trust the situation or rely

on either parent for stability. It makes them feel divided—they can never share the good times with the other parent. It makes them feel apprehensive—they can never count on their parents to behave appropriately. They live in constant fear of embarrassment, humiliation or physical harm.

In high conflict situations, the child is placed in the middle and must spend enormous amounts of energy adapting to and mediating between their parents. Any child who is exposed to ongoing conflict does not have the freedom to develop his or her own personality and positive self image. Some mental health professionals believe that ongoing high conflict is a form of child abuse. It is an unnecessary tragedy.

- **Alienation**
  Alienation happens when one parent turns the children against the other. Whether it's intentional or unintentional, subtle or overt, it is destructive because it robs the children of their right to freely love each parent. And, in extreme cases, it robs the children of a parent.

- **Abandonment**
  The pressures and pain of a divorce cause some parents to leave. They may go on to establish a wonderful life—new spouse or partner, new job, even new kids. It is absolutely not wonderful for the children who are left behind. They must cope with the devastating reality that they have been rejected and abandoned.

  This rejection burns an unrelenting hole in their souls that affects every aspect of their being for their entire life. While these children may find success in their adult lives, they are haunted by the knowledge that their parent did not care enough to stay with them. Abandonment causes permanent scars. Never discount its effect.

- **Abuse or Domestic Violence**
  Children who are victims of physical, emotional or sexual abuse or who witness domestic violence learn what they are taught. Everything they witness becomes their truth and their reality. These unfortunate children must completely relearn acceptable and

normal behavior. It is extremely difficult. Some children never recover. Often, the abused become the abusers.

What Are the Best Things that You Can Do for Your Children (and Guarantee Success in the Process)?

Fortunately, my list of "best" things exceeds my "worst" list. Children benefit from many things. But the top ten things that bring them happiness and success include:

- **Unconditional Love**
  Before all else, children need the unconditional love of their parents. It is a fundamental and driving requirement of life. Without it, they become lost.

  But, there is another side to this coin. Just as children need the unconditional love of their parents, they also need to be able to give love. So, be a receptive parent. Don't build a wall around yourself and shut the children out. Unless there are significant problems, encourage and support their loving relationship with the other parent. Give your children permission to give love as well as to receive it.

- **Parents Who Are Parents**

  Parenting is a humbling experience. It is an art. If you haven't fully participated in parenting your children and you want to do that, don't be embarrassed to ask for help. There are many age-appropriate classes that you can take through local organizations.

  Parenting is a challenge under the best of circumstances. Parenting after divorce can be overwhelming. Just let people (including the other parent) know that you need some assistance. Keep asking until someone provides answers and help.

- **Freedom to Just Be Kids**

  A divorce does not change the needs of children. They must have the time and space to be kids—to run idly through the park, to jump in a pile of leaves, to play, to dream, to make mistakes and to love. Don't ask them to assume responsibilities that are unreasonable. They cannot be your friend. They cannot assume the role of the absent parent. Let your children be free to savor the joys and meet the challenges of childhood.

- **Permission to Grieve and
  Express Their Emotions**
  The loss of an intact family is as
  significant to your children as the divorce
  is to you. The family, as they have known
  it, disappears. Just like adults, children
  must grieve this loss in order to heal.
  This means that they, too, will feel
  depressed, angry and sad.

  As a parent, you must allow your
  children to grieve at their own speed.
  You must acknowledge and help them
  with their emotions. Get professional
  counseling or find a support group for
  them. It is one more challenge, but your
  children probably didn't want the divorce,
  and they will need your help to adjust.

- **Security**
  Children do not have a very good
  perspective on life. They only understand
  what they observe. They lack the
  experience and knowledge to conclude
  that tomorrow will be different from
  today. So, if their mother dissolves in tears
  because the child support did not arrive,
  or if their father becomes infuriated
  because the parenting time was withheld,

the children may easily conclude that this will be the pattern for the rest of their lives will overwhelm them.

As a parent, you need to provide security for your children. They must be able to rely on you. Let them see, by your words and actions, that you will behave predictably and reasonably. Separate your children from the harsh reality of the divorce. Communicate with them carefully, lovingly and frequently. Reassure them that the difficulties will be resolved—then follow through. It is the only way that your children can focus on the main objective of their small existence—to grow up!

- **Food and Necessities**
The financial needs of the children do not stop when you get divorced. By law, each parent has a duty to support his or her children. It can be an overwhelming task, but it may not be excused. No matter how tough it gets, keep working on it. Sometimes parents must cooperate and help each other put food on the table. Don't hesitate. You might not even get thanked. But, you will give your

children the gift of financial security.
Make it happen!

- **Education**

  A divorce does not let you off the hook.
  To raise strong independent children, you
  must educate them. This means that you
  must establish or continue your role as a
  teacher. Help your children with their
  homework, and get involved with their
  school. Make sure that they know how to
  read and write. Make sure that they
  know their math. And, oh yes, make sure
  that you teach them to respect
  themselves and others, to take
  responsibility for their actions and
  decisions, to be honest, to cooperate, to
  keep commitments, and to love and
  sacrifice. Your children will thank you,
  their most important teacher.

- **Rules and Boundaries**

  Children need boundaries. They need to
  follow the rules. The problem is, a
  divorce may cause your expectations to
  get muddled. So, set reasonable
  boundaries for your children. If you

change the rules, tell the children and help them understand. Let them know what is expected of them. Be consistent and predictable in your enforcement. It makes them feel more secure because they know that you are in charge.

- **Both Parents**
  Don't let your emotions get in the way of your common sense. Children need both parents even in the most extreme and abusive cases. You may need to structure the parenting time to provide for the children's safety, but don't make them choose between their parents. You can cause great pain to the other parent by withholding or manipulating the children. But, the temporary satisfaction you might gain will rob the children of their right to love and be loved by both of their parents. It is a very high price to exact from innocent bystanders—the children.

- **Role Models**
  Remember the old adage that the apple doesn't fall far from the tree? Your

children will grow up to be like you—
and that can be a very scary thought.
So, set a good example. Treat other
people (especially the other parent) like
you want to be treated. You will reap
great rewards!

> **Make sure that you don't follow the worst list. Instead, embrace and follow the best list.**

Chapter 13

Divorce Etiquette

Are There Rules We Can Follow that Will Make Our Lives Easier?

YES! The landscape of divorce is a slippery slope, and you must traverse it carefully if you want to create a healthy *Post-Divorce Family*. Like every other part of your life, there are guidelines or etiquette that you might consider. Why? They will make your life infinitely easier. Here they are:

- **Recognize That You May Be Out of Sync with the Other Parent**
  Understand that the other parent might be months if not years behind you in his or her adjustment to the reality of the divorce. This is not unusual. Often, one parent has been considering a divorce for years and is ready to move on—and move on fast! This other is still grieving

the loss of the relationship and is in an
enormous amount of pain. For the sake
of the children, be respectful of this
difference. Believe it or not, it's not all
about you!

- **Don't Rush the Introductions**
  Keep new boyfriends/girlfriends out of
  the picture for a while. Let the children
  adjust. Don't kick the other parent under
  the bus by introducing a new "friend"
  to the children. Have the good sense
  to wait.

- **Treat the Other Parent with Respect**
  Many divorced couples treat their
  employees with more respect than they
  treat the other parent. Yet, the job that has
  been entrusted to that person (raising the
  children) is far more important than any
  other in your life. So, treat the other
  parent like a business partner, and give
  him or her all the respect that the
  position demands. Do this even if you
  think they have not earned your respect.
  Your children will understand and
  appreciate. Your *Post-Divorce Family* will
  remain intact.

- **Be Honest**

  Be forthright and honest—disclose all of your assets and income. This may sound silly since the law requires such disclosure. However, more than one couple has spent thousands of dollars to find hidden money. In the end, it is usually not cost effective, and it totally erodes trust. Remember, after all is said and done, you still have to raise the kids together. It's pretty hard to do that constructively if you have tried to hoodwink the other parent.

- **Divulge Relationship Information**

  Your life is private after a divorce. You have no obligation to give the other parent any information about your private life. Right? Wrong—if you have kids.

  It's never fair to the new person in your life, to your children and to the other parent to fail to inform the other parent if you are in a serious relationship. Let the other parent know if you will be inviting the children to your wedding. Is it his or her business? Yes, because it affects the children. And, it sends a message to the children that, regardless of how things have changed, their parents still love them and are still working together to make sure they are safe. It helps them feel secure during a very wobbly time.

- **Share Requests**
  Let the other parent know if you want to take the children on a special vacation that will conflict with their school schedules or the other parent's *Parenting Time*. Should you tell your child about your vacation plans before you tell the other parent??? Definitely not a good idea!

- **Listen to the children**
  Encourage your children to speak about their concerns. However, let them know that you will be sharing the information with the other parent. If your child knows that you are still working with and talking to the other parent, the child is less likely to play you against the other or manipulate you to gain an advantage. Unless the child is divulging incidents of abuse, be very careful about keeping secrets.

- **Save the Criticism**
  Don't criticize the other parent if the
  children are in the house or in ear
  shot. Although they may not be in
  the same room, they will hear you.
  They don't need to be privy to adult
  conversations, and they don't want
  to hear personal details about your
  relationship with their father or mother.
  As one child said, "If you hate
  Mom, you must hate me because I'm
  half Mom."

- **Spare the Children**
  Don't feel compelled to tell the children
  all of the gory details of the divorce. This
  is true even if your former wife or
  husband was unfaithful. Perhaps in the
  end, you will come to understand that
  you also contributed to the breakup.
  Giving the children only one side of the
  facts is misleading to them and
  destructive. You have a different
  perspective from the other parent, and it
  is unnecessary to place the children in a
  position of having to "side" with one
  parent or the other.

- **Share Medical Information**
  Be sure to keep the other parent informed if your child is ill or is having difficulty of any sort. This sounds so basic, but, if you have been put down or criticized by the other parent, you will find that it's much easier to say, "screw him (or her)," and keep him/her out of a portion of the child's life. Don't do it—even if the other parent has done it to you. Just keep your child in your mind and communicate for your kid.

- **Don't Keep Secrets**
  This is a difficult issue. A child may tell you something in confidence that reveals a dangerous situation that exists in the other parent's home. Your child needs to confide in a parent but specifically asks you not to discuss it with the other parent. This is always a problem, and parents handle it on a case by case basis. If it is necessary to confront the other parent in order to protect your child, tell your child that you will be sharing the information. Better yet, establish a rule with the other parent and your children that prohibits secrets—everything must be on the table and confronted. This

actually takes the pressure off the children because they know that they can discuss problems with both parents.

- **Don't Assume That Your Children Will Tell the Truth**
  Kids will go to great lengths to feel safe with each parent and to protect their parents. Sometimes they lie. Sometimes they tell half of the truth to one parent and the other half to the other parent. Sometimes they misinterpret a situation. Listen with both ears when your child speaks to you. Don't jump to conclusions about the other parent. Check it out. You may be surprised.

- **Always Focus on Your *Post-Divorce Family***
  Remember your *Family Mission Statement*? Remember that your *Post-Divorce Family* comes first. You're a package deal, and new *significant others* must accept the whole deal…not just the most convenient or thrilling part. Stay away from new mates who can't stand your children or hate the other parent. It's unlikely that their attitude will change, and it's just not worth it.

Chapter 14

Parting Thoughts

The Truth from My Perspective

When two people have children, they create an inextricable bond that will be changed, but not broken, by divorce or separation. The challenge is to define the change, commit to your parental responsibilities, and create a healthy and loving environment for your children. Use your *Parenting Plan* to help you. It will save you thousands of hours of stress, and it will become the glue that enables your children to transition from the pain of their shattered world to the joy of a successful *Post-Divorce Family*. Cooperative parenting is the greatest gift you can give your children.

I do not believe that divorced parents get enough credit for facing and resolving the challenges of coparenting after divorce. Tenacity, bravery, patience, strength, and uncompromising love are a few of the terms that describe this remarkable feat.

Additionally, I do not believe that we give our children of divorce enough credit. It's easy to say that children are resilient and that "they will get over it." It's easy to say that "if the parents are ok, the children will be ok." I respectfully disagree. Your children may experience guilt, grief, parental conflict, abandonment, alienation, and loss of their innocent childhood. They will become divided—physically, financially, emotionally and intellectually. And, if the divorce is contentious, they will be interviewed by a myriad of experts, which can be amazingly intrusive.

But—it is entirely possible for your children to benefit from your divorce. They may actually find the separation somewhat of a relief if you and the other parent have had angry exchanges. With your help, your kids can develop strength and endurance. They may be able to forge a new relationship with a previously absent parent who, as a result of the divorce, becomes more active in their lives. If allowed and appropriate, they will be able to find their voice and share their ideas and perspectives with you. It's challenging work, and your children deserve credit too!

When I was divorced in the early 1970s, there was no such thing as joint custody (much less shared decision-making). Developing a creative *Parenting Plan* that accommodated the children's needs, the parent's needs, and the *Post-Divorce Family* was un-heard of at that time.

This has changed, and you have the opportunity to take full advantage of all the lessons that have been learned by parents who went before you. Still, parenting after divorce is just plain challenging. Are you ready? If so, then, give yourself and your children a hug. And—don't stop!

PART FOUR

Resources

Chapter 15

I Need Help!

Where Should I Go?

There are many people and organizations that can help you step through your divorce. If you need legal assistance, you might call your state Bar Association for lawyer referrals or your state or local legal aid society if you have a low income. The names of collaborative lawyers can be found on line or from the International Academy of Collaborative Professionals. Local lawyers from national groups such as the American Academy of Matrimonial Attorneys can also be of enormous help.

You can get referrals for private mediators from your state Bar Association, a mediation organization in your state, or listings in your Yellow Pages. You can also get names in your state from *www.My.SuperLawyers.com* or *www.BestLawyers.com*.

Religious organizations often provide divorce support groups/classes or could refer you to such activities. You might also check with the YMCA or other local recreation associations.

If you would like to work with a therapist, you can call your state or local mental health association or get a referral from your doctor, your lawyer or your mediator.

Don't underestimate the information you can get from the Internet, but check it out. Not everything you will find will be reliable.

How about Other Resources?

Children's Books

Here are some children's books that are beautifully written and easy to share with your kids:

- *We're Having A Tuesday,* by D.K. Simoneau, AC Publications Group, 2006.
- *Was It the Chocolate Pudding: A Story for Little Kids About Divorce,* by Sandra Levins and Bryan Langdo, American Psychological Assn., 2005.
- *KoKo Doll Divorce Book,* by Vicki Lansky, Jane Prince, and Vicki L. Lansky, The Book Peddlers, 1999.
- *Standing on My Own Two Feet: A Child's Affirmation of Love in the Midst of Divorce*, by Tamara Schmitz, Price Stern Sloan, 2008.
- *Dinosaurs Divorce,* by Marc Brown and Laurie Krasny Brown, Little, Brown Books for Young Readers, 1988.
- *What in the World Do You Do When Your Parents Divorce? A Survival Guide for Kids,* by Kent Winchester J.D. and Roberta Beyer, J.D., Free Spirit Publishing, 2001.

- *Divorce is Not the End of the World: Zoe's and Evan's Coping Guide for Kids,* by Zoe Stern and Evan Stern, Tricycle Press, 1997.
- *Hope No Matter What: Helping Your Children Heal After Divorce,* by Kim Hill and Lisa Harper, Regal, 2008.

Adult Books

There are many books on divorce, and here are some good ones:

- *Mom's House, Dad's House,* by Isolina Ricci, Ph.D., Fireside, revised edition, 1997.
- *Mom's House, Dad's House for Kids,* by Isolina Ricci, Ph.D., Fireside, 2006.
- *The CoParenting Toolkit: 7 Secrets for Success,* by Isolina Ricci, Ph.D., CoParentingToday Publications, 2011.
- *In the Name of the Child,* by Janet R. Johnston, Ph.D. and Vivienne Roseby, Ph.D., Free Press, 1997.
- *Through the Eyes of Children: Healing Stories for Children of Divorce,* by Janet R. Johnston, Ph.D., Karen Breunig, M.S., Carla Garrity, Ph.D., and Mitchell Baris, Ph.D., Free Press, 1997.
- *How to Help Your Child Overcome Your Divorce* by Elissa P. Benedek, M.D. and Catherine F. Brown, Newmarket Press, second edition, 2001.
- *The Dollars and Sense of Divorce,* by Judith Briles, Carol Ann Wilson, Edward Schilling III, Kaplan Business, 1998.
- *Divorce Book for Parents,* by Vicki Lansky, The Book Peddlers, 3rd edition, 1996.

- *Helping Children Cope With Divorce* , by Edward Teyber, Ph.D., Jossey-Bass, revised, 2001.
- *Crazy Time: Surviving Divorce & Building a New Life*, by Abigail Trafford, Harper Perennial, revised edition, 1992.
- *How to Divorce as Friends* , by Bill Ferguson, Return to the Heart, 2001.
- *The Truth About Children and Divorce: Dealing With the Emotions So You and Your Children Can Thrive*, by Robert E. Emery, Ph.D., Plume, 2006.
- *Custody Chaos, Personal Peace: Sharing Custody With an Ex Who Drives You Crazy*, by Jeffrey P. Wittman, Perigee Trade, 2001.
- *Surviving the Breakup: How Children and Parents Cope With Divorce*, by Judith S. Wallerstein, Ph.D. and Joan B. Kelly, Ph.D., Basic Books, 1996.
- *Between Two Worlds: The Inner Lives of Children of Divorce*, by Elizabeth Marquardt, Three Rivers Press, 2006.
- *In Two Happy Homes*, by Shirley Thomas, Ph.D., Springboard Publications, 2005.
- *Ordinary Issues - Extraordinary Solutions: A Legal Guide for the Colorado GLBT Community*, by Kimberly R. Willoughby, Bradford Publishing Company, 2003.
- *The Special Needs Child and Divorce*, by Margaret "Pegi" S. Price, American Bar Association, 2009.

Online Resources

You will find amazing tools on line. The ones listed below are particularly good:

- *www.CoParentingToday.com*—*A free website for co-parents that includes a series of helpful articles and a lesson plan for school-based groups.*
- *www.UpToParents.org*—A free, confidential website for divorcing and divorced parents.
- *www.ProudToParent.org*—A free, confidential website for parents who were never married to each other.
- *www.OurFamilyWizard.com*—An online custody calendar and information manager that allows easy scheduling and tracking of parenting time. Yearly fee.
- *www.CoFamilies.com*—A free web calendar for co-parents, step parents and blended families.
- *www.DivorceandChildren.com*—Online articles and help for both children and parents.
- *www.DivorceAsFriends.com*—Articles, resources and support to help minimize conflict and possibly save the marriage.

Articles

- Cashmore and Parkinson, (January 2008). *Children's and Parent's Perceptions on Children's Participation in Decision Making After Parent Separation and Divorce,* 46 Family Court Review 1.
- McIntosh *et al,* (January 2008), *Child-Focused and Child-Inclusive Divorce Mediation: Comparative Outcomes From a Prospective Study of Postseparation Adjustment.* 46 Family Court Review 1.
- McWilliams and Hinds, (October 2008), *Child-Inclusive Divorce: 2008 Colorado Family Law Survey,* 37 Colo. Lawyer 10.

- Meierding, (May 28, 2008), *Children in the Mediation Process, Association of Family and Conciliation Courts Annual Conference,* Vancouver, British Columbia.
- Parkinson and Cashmore, (2007), "What Responsibility Do Courts Have to Hear Children's Voices?" 15 Int'l J. of Children's Rights 43.

Acknowledgments

It's always a pleasure to give credit where credit is due. My two daughters have been my inspiration for this book (and for many parts of my life). As adult children of divorce, they have created great success in their lives. They are devoted mothers, and they are raising their children to be responsible and loving participants in life.

Credit also goes to my dear husband, my extraordinary son-in-law, my amazing grandchildren, my family, and my extended family members, each of whom has contributed greatly to my happiness and success.

I am indebted to my colleagues. They have generously shared their ideas, their wise suggestions, and their thoughtful solutions. I have grown from those friendships.

Special thanks to Dr. Judith Briles, The Book Shepherd, whose determined advice and counsel lifted this book from a draft on my desk to a finished product.

Finally, there are my clients. They come to mediation at a time of crisis. Our lives cross for a brief period of time, and, hopefully, we each leave the mediation with new ideas and a new approach to life.

To all, I thank you.

Joan

About the Author

Joan McWilliams is a pioneer in the field of mediation. She conducts a full-time dispute resolution practice in domestic and commercial conflicts through her firm, McWilliams Mediation Group Ltd. Before starting her mediation practice over twenty years ago, she served as a law clerk for the Tenth Circuit Court of Appeals and was a partner in a large Denver law firm.

Joan is the creator of the *Post-Divorce Family Model*™ that she uses in mediation when children are involved in a divorce. She has been an adjunct professor at the University Of Denver College Of Law, active in the Colorado and Denver Bar Associations, a co-initiator of the Colorado Parental Responsibilities Bill and an Advanced Practitioner Member of the Association for Conflict Resolution. The University Of Denver College Of Law honored her with its prestigious Alumni Professionalism Award. She received the Family Law Icon Award from the Colorado Bar Association. AV Rated, Joan is listed in *The Best Lawyers in America, Super Lawyers 5280 and U.S. News—Best Lawyers/Best Law Firms.* She is the author of the award-winning book, *The Peace Finder: Riley McFee's Quest for World Peace,* and *Creating Parenting Plans That Work.*

Joan McWilliams can be reached for consultations and speaking at:

> **303.830.0171 (phone), 303.830.8422 (fax)**
> **Joan@McWilliamsMediation.com**
> **www.McWilliamsMediation.com**
> **McWilliams Mediation Group Ltd**
> **P.O. Box 6216**
> **Denver, CO 80206**